EVIDENCE-BASED TREATMENT PLANNING FOR GENERALIZED ANXIETY DISORDER

EVIDENCE-BASED TREATMENT PLANNING FOR GENERALIZED ANXIETY DISORDER

DVD FACILITATOR'S GUIDE

TIMOTHY J. BRUCE
AND
ARTHUR E. JONGSMA, JR.

John Wiley & Sons, Inc.

Contents

Introduction

This *Facilitator's Guide* is designed to help you lead an educational training session in *Evidence-Based Treatment Planning for Generalized Anxiety Disorder*. It is to be used in conjunction with the DVD and its *Companion Workbook*. The *Guide* walks you through the process of delivering a training session.

The training session should be conducted in a comfortable room, where participants can read and write in their workbooks. A DVD player and monitor are required.

Organization

In this *Guide* you will find in each chapter:

➤ Chapter review questions and answers
➤ Chapter review test questions and answers
➤ Talking points—this feature presents an optional question with a highlighted point or points to include in the discussion
➤ Chapter references

In appropriate chapters the references are divided into those for *empirical support*, those for *clinical resources*, and those for *bibliotherapy resources*. Empirical support references are selected studies or reviews of the empirical work supporting the efficacy of the empirically supported treatments (ESTs) discussed in the chapter. The clinical resources are books, manuals, or other resources for clinicians that describe the application, or "how to," of the treatments discussed. The bibliotherapy resources are selected publications and Web sites relevant to the DVD content that may be helpful to clinicians, clients, or laypersons.

Examples of client homework are included at www.wiley.com/go/gadwb They are designed to enhance understanding of therapeutic interventions, in addition to being potentially useful clinically.

Appendix A contains an example of an evidence-based treatment plan for Generalized Anxiety Disorder. In Appendix B, correct and incorrect answers to all chapter review test questions are explained.

Chapter Points

This DVD is electronically marked with chapter points that delineate the beginning of major sections throughout the program. You may skip to any one of these chapter points on the DVD by clicking on the forward arrow. The chapter points for this program are as follows:

- Defining Generalized Anxiety Disorder
- Six Steps in Building a Psychotherapy Treatment Plan
- Brief History of the EST Movement
- ESTs for Generalized Anxiety Disorder
- Integrating ESTs for Generalized Anxiety Disorder Into a Treatment Plan
- Common Considerations in Relapse Prevention
- An Evidence-Based Treatment Plan for Generalized Anxiety Disorder

Series Rationale

Evidence-based practice (EBP) is steadily becoming the standard of mental health care as it has in medical health care. Borrowing from the Institute of Medicine's definition (Institute of Medicine, 2001), the American Psychological Association (APA) has defined EBP as "the integration of the best available research with clinical expertise in the context of patient characteristics, culture, and preferences" (American Psychological Association Presidential Task Force on Evidence-Based Practice (APA), 2006).

Professional organizations such as the American Psychological Association, the National Association of Social Workers, and the American Psychiatric Association, as well as consumer organizations such as the National Alliance for the Mentally Ill (NAMI), are endorsing EBP. At the federal level, a major joint initiative of the National Institute of Mental Health and Department of Health and Human Services' Substance Abuse and Mental Health Services Administration (SAMHSA) focuses on promoting, implementing, and evaluating evidence-based mental health programs and practices within state mental health systems (APA, 2006). In some practice settings, EBP is even becoming mandated. It is clear that the call for evidence-based practice is being increasingly sounded.

Unfortunately, many mental health care providers cannot or do not stay abreast of results from clinical research and how they can inform their practices. Although it has rightfully been argued that the relevance of some research to the clinician's needs is weak, there are products of clinical research whose efficacy has been well established and whose effectiveness in the community setting has received support. Clinicians and clinicians-in-training interested in empirically informing their treatments could benefit from educational programs that make this goal more easily attainable.

This series of DVDs and companion workbooks is designed to introduce clinicians and students to the process of empirically informing their psychotherapy treatment plans. The series begins with an introduction to the efforts to identify research-supported treatments and how the products of these efforts can be used to inform treatment planning. The other programs in the series focus on empirically informed treatment planning for each of several commonly seen clinical problems. In each problem-focused DVD, issues involved in defining or diagnosing the presenting problem are reviewed. Research-supported treatments for the problem are described, as well as the process used to identify them. Viewers are then systematically guided through the process of creating a treatment plan, and shown how the plan can be informed by goals, objectives, and interventions consistent with those of the identified research-supported treatments. Example vignettes of selected interventions are also provided.

This series is intended to be educational and informative in nature and not meant to be a substitute for clinical training in the specific interventions discussed and demonstrated. References to empirical support of the treatments described, clinical resource material, and training opportunities are provided.

Presenters

Dr. Art Jongsma is the Series Editor and co-author of the Practice*Planners*® series published by John Wiley & Sons. He has authored or co-authored more than 40 books in this series. Among the books included in this series are the highly regarded *The Complete Adult Psychotherapy Treatment Planner*, *The Adolescent* and *The Child Psychotherapy Treatment Planners*, and *The Addiction Treatment Planner*. All of these books, along with *The Severe and Persistent Mental Illness Treatment Planner*, *The Family Therapy Treatment Planner*, *The Couples Psychotherapy Treatment Planner*, *The Older Adult Psychotherapy Treatment Planner*, and *The Veterans and Active Duty Military Psychotherapy Treatment Planner*, are informed with Objectives and Interventions that are supported by research evidence.

Dr. Jongsma also created the clinical record management software tool Thera*Scribe*®, which uses point-and-click technology to easily develop, store,

Exhibit I.1   Dr. Tim Bruce and Dr. Art Jongsma

and print treatment plans, progress notes, and homework assignments. He has conducted treatment planning and software training workshops for mental health professionals around the world.

Dr. Jongsma's clinical career began as a psychologist in a large private psychiatric hospital. After working in the hospital for about 10 years, he then transitioned to outpatient work in his own private practice clinic, Psychological Consultants, in Grand Rapids, Michigan, for 25 years. He has been writing best-selling books and software for mental health professionals since 1995. He lives in a suburb of Grand Rapids with his wife, Judy.

Dr. Timothy Bruce is a Professor and Associate Chair of the Department of Psychiatry and Behavioral Medicine at the University of Illinois, College of Medicine in Peoria, Illinois, where he also directs medical student education. He is a licensed clinical psychologist who completed his graduate training at SUNY-Albany under the mentorship of Dr. David Barlow and his residency training at Wilford Hall Medical Center under the direction of Dr. Robert Klepac. In addition to maintaining an active clinical practice at the university, Dr. Bruce has written numerous publications, including books, professional journal articles, book chapters, and professional educational materials, many on the topic of evidence-based practice. Most recently, he has served as the developmental editor empirically informing Dr. Jongsma's best-selling Practice*Planners*® series.

Dr. Bruce is also Executive Director of the Center for the Dissemination of Evidence-based Mental Health Practices, a state- and federally funded initiative to disseminate evidence-based psychological and pharmacological practices across Illinois. Highly recognized as an educator, Dr. Bruce has received nearly thirty awards for his teaching of students and professionals during his career.

References

American Psychological Association Presidential Task Force on Evidence-Based Practice. (2006). Evidence-based practice in psychology. *American Psychologist, 61*, 271–185.

Berghuis, D., Jongsma, A., & Bruce, T. (2006). *The severe and persistent mental illness treatment planner* (2nd ed.). Hoboken, NJ: Wiley.

Dattilio, F., Jongsma, A., & Davis, S. (2009). *The family therapy treatment planner* (2nd ed.). Hoboken, NJ: Wiley.

Institute of Medicine. (2001). *Crossing the quality chasm: A new health system for the 21st century.* Washington, DC: National Academy Press.

Jongsma, A., Peterson, M., & Bruce, T. (2006). *The complete adult psychotherapy treatment planner* (4th ed.). Hoboken, NJ: Wiley.

Jongsma, A., Peterson, M., McInnis, W., & Bruce, T. (2006a). *The adolescent psychotherapy treatment planner* (4th ed.). Hoboken, NJ: Wiley.

Jongsma, A., Peterson, M., McInnis, W., & Bruce, T. (2006b). *The child psychotherapy treatment planner* (4th ed.). Hoboken, NJ: Wiley.

Moore, B., & Jongsma, A. (2009). *The veterans and active duty military psychotherapy treatment planner.* Hoboken, NJ: Wiley.

Perkinson, R., Jongsma, A., & Bruce, T. (2009). *The addiction treatment planner* (4th ed.). Hoboken, NJ: Wiley.

What Is Generalized Anxiety Disorder?

Chapter Review

1. What is Generalized Anxiety Disorder?

Generalized Anxiety Disorder *DSM–IV* Diagnostic Criteria

A. Excessive anxiety and worry, occurring more days than not, for a period of at least six months, and is focused on a number of events or activities

Examples of adult worries in GAD:
- Daily responsibilities
- Health of family members
- Safety of children
- Finances
- Job security
- Relationships

Theme of childhood worries in GAD:
- Quality or competence of behavioral performance at home or in school

B. Difficulty controlling the worry

C. Three or more additional symptoms, including:
- Restlessness or feeling keyed up or on edge
- Being easily fatigued
- Difficulty concentrating or going blank
- Irritability
- Muscle tension
- Sleep disturbance

(continued)

> D. The worry in GAD should not represent the feature of another psychiatric disorder.
>
> E. The anxiety, worry, or physical symptoms of GAD must cause clinically significant distress or functional impairment.
>
> F. Symptoms of GAD are not caused by the direct physiological effects of a substance or a general medical condition.

Chapter Review Test Questions

1. Which of the following best describes the primary diagnostic feature of Generalized Anxiety Disorder (GAD)?

   A. Excessive worry specifically about being humiliated in public

   B. Excessive worry about several everyday or real-life problems

   C. Excessive worry about having a specific disease

   D. Excessive worry specifically about having an unexpected panic attack

   Answer: B

2. True or false? According to the *DSM*, you can diagnose Generalized Anxiety Disorder when only the excessive worry criteria are met; that is, without any evidence of physiological overarousal.

   Answer: False

Talking Points

As noted in the chapter, generalized anxiety disorder (GAD) is characterized by excessive worry about numerous real-life circumstances, yet worry is ubiquitous in the general population (i.e., everyone worries). To distinguish excessive worry from normal worry, diagnostic criteria place an emphasis on the frequency (i.e., "occurring more days than not") and chronicity (i.e., "for at least six months"). However, worry occurs in some other mental disorders and is not supposed to be diagnosed separately as GAD. Consider facilitating a discussion about common differential diagnoses in which "worry" occurs but is not considered GAD. You could ask the question "In what other mental disorders do you see excessive worry?" The following is a guide from criteria D in the *DSM* criteria for GAD:

- The focus of the anxiety and worry is not confined to features of an Axis I disorder, for example:
  - The anxiety or worry is not about having a Panic Attack (as in Panic Disorder)
  - Being embarrassed in public (as in Social Phobia)
  - Being contaminated (as in Obsessive-Compulsive Disorder)
  - Being away from home or close relatives (as in Separation Anxiety Disorder)
  - Gaining weight (as in Anorexia Nervosa)
  - Having multiple physical complaints (as in Somatization Disorder)
  - Having a serious illness (as in Hypochondriasis)

Chapter Reference

American Psychiatric Association. (2000). *Diagnostic and statistical manual of mental disorders* (4th ed., text rev.; DSM-IV-TR). Washington, DC: American Psychiatric Association.

CHAPTER 2

What Are the Six Steps in Building a Treatment Plan?

Chapter Review

1. What are the six steps involved in developing a psychotherapy treatment plan?

Six Steps in Building a Psychotherapy Treatment Plan

Step 1: Identify primary and secondary problems

Step 2: Describe the problem's behavioral manifestations (symptom pattern)

Step 3: Make a diagnosis based on *DSM/ICD* criteria

Step 4: Specify long-term goals

Step 5: Create short-term objectives

Step 6: Select therapeutic interventions

Key Point

One important aspect of effective treatment planning is that each plan should be tailored to the individual client's particular problems and needs. Treatment plans should not be boilerplate, even if clients have similar problems. Consistent with the definition of an evidence-based practice, the individual's strengths and weaknesses, unique stressors, cultural and social network, family circumstances, and symptom patterns must be considered in developing a treatment strategy. Clinicians should rely on their own good clinical judgment and plan a treatment that is appropriate for the distinctive individual with whom they are working.

Chapter Review Test Questions

1. Some patients with Generalized Anxiety Disorder (GAD) may worry about finances or job security. Others may worry about their children or deadlines.

Some may have a sleep disturbance, whereas others may not. In which step of treatment planning would you record the particular expressions of GAD for your individual client?

A. Creating short-term objectives
B. Describing the problem's manifestations
C. Identifying the primary problem
D. Selecting treatment interventions

Answer: B

2. The statement "Learn and implement problem-solving skills to address worries in a more productive manner" is an example of a statement describing which of the following elements of a psychotherapy treatment plan?

A. A primary problem
B. A short-term objective
C. A symptom manifestation
D. A treatment intervention

Answer: B

Talking Point

What is the relationship between short-term objectives (STOs) and treatment interventions (TIs) in a psychotherapy treatment plan?

- In short, STOs are desired actions of the client, while TIs are the therapist's actions designed to help clients achieve their objectives.

Chapter References

American Psychological Association Presidential Task Force on Evidence-Based Practice. (2006). Evidence-based practice in psychology. *American Psychologist, 61*, 271–185.

Jongsma, A. (2005). Psychotherapy treatment plan writing. In G. P. Koocher, J. C. Norcross, and S. S. Hill (Eds.), *Psychologists' desk reference* (2nd ed., pp. 232–236). New York, NY: Oxford University Press.

Jongsma, A., Peterson, M., & Bruce, T. (2006). *The complete adult psychotherapy treatment planner* (4th ed.). Hoboken, NJ: Wiley.

Jongsma, A., Peterson, M., McInnis, W., & Bruce, T. (2006). *The adolescent psychotherapy treatment planner* (4th ed.). Hoboken, NJ: Wiley.

3

What Is the Brief History of the Empirically Supported Treatments Movement?

Chapter Review

1. How did Division 12 of the APA identify ESTs?

> Task group reviewers evaluated the psychotherapy outcome literature to identify treatments whose efficacy had been supported through empirical study. Two primary sets of criteria were used to judge the evidence base supporting any particular therapy. One was termed *well-established*, the other *probably efficacious*.

2. What are the primary differences between *well-established* and *probably efficacious* criteria used to identify ESTs?

> - The criteria for a well-established treatment required at least two randomized, placebo-controlled trials (RCTs), or two randomized trials comparing the treatment to an already established treatment, or a large series of single-case design studies. In these studies, treatment manuals had to be used, and characteristics of the client sample had to be specified. Finally, replication by independent investigators had to have been demonstrated.
> - The criteria for a probably efficacious treatment could be met with two demonstrations of efficacy over a wait-list control. This is a lower level of evidence than for a well-established treatment; it rules out only that the condition being treated does not remit on its own.
> - Alternatively, one or more randomized, placebo-controlled trials or randomized trials comparing the treatment to an already established treatment in which manuals were used, client characteristics were specified, but independent replication had *not* been demonstrated would suffice.
> - As with the well-established criteria, a single-case series, but of smaller size than required for well-established, could be used.
>
> See Figure 3.1 for use if more detailed questions arise.

Figure 3.1

Specific Criteria for Well-Established and Probably Efficacious Treatments

Criteria for a Well-Established Treatment

For a psychological treatment to be considered *well-established*, the evidence base supporting it had to be characterized by the following:

I. At least two good between-group design experiments demonstrating efficacy in one or more of the following ways:

    A. Superior (statistically significantly so) to pill or psychological placebo or to another treatment

    B. Equivalent to an already established treatment in experiments with adequate sample sizes

OR

II. A large series of single-case design experiments (n > 9) demonstrating efficacy. These experiments must have:

    A. Used good experimental designs

    B. Compared the intervention to another treatment as in IA

Further Criteria for Both I and II

III. Experiments must be conducted with treatment manuals.

IV. Characteristics of the client samples must be clearly specified.

V. Effects must have been demonstrated by at least two different investigators or investigating teams.

Criteria for a Probably Efficacious Treatment

For a psychological treatment to be considered *probably efficacious*, the evidence base supporting it had to meet the following criteria:

I. Two experiments showing the treatment is superior (statistically significantly so) to a waiting-list control group.

OR

II. One or more experiments meeting the Well-Established Treatment Criteria IA or IB, III, and IV, but not V.

OR

III. A small series of single-case design experiments (n > 3) otherwise meeting Well-Established Treatment.

Adapted from "Update on Empirically Validated Therapies, II," by D. L. Chambless, M. J. Baker, D. H. Baucom, L. E. Beutler, K. S. Calhoun, P. Crits-Christoph, . . . S. R. Woody, 1998, *The Clinical Psychologist*, 51(1), 3–16.

Key Point

Division 12's criteria for a well-established treatment are similar to the standards used by the United States Food and Drug Administration (FDA) to evaluate the safety and efficacy of proposed medications. The FDA requires demonstration that a proposed medication is significantly superior to a nonspecific control treatment (a pill placebo) in at least two randomized controlled trials conducted by independent research groups. Division 12's criteria for a well-established treatment require the equivalent of this standard as well as other features relevant to judging a psychological treatment's efficacy (e.g., a clear description of the treatment and study participants). By extension, if the FDA were to evaluate psychotherapies using the criteria they use for medication, it would allow sale of those judged to be well-established.

---

3. Where can information about ESTs and evidence-based practices be found?

- The Society of Clinical Psychology, Division 12, maintains the growing list of research-supported psychological treatments at: http://www.psychologicaltreatments.org

- Descriptions of the treatments identified through many of the early EST reviews, as well as references to the empirical work supporting them, clinical resources, and training opportunities, can be found at www.therapyadvisor.com. This resource was developed by Personal Improvement Computer Systems (PICS) with funding from the National Institute of Mental Health and in consultation with members of the original Division 12 task groups. Information found on Therapyadvisor is provided by the primary author/researcher(s) of the given EST.

- Great Britain is at the forefront of the effort to identify evidence-based treatments and develop guidelines for practice. The latest products of their work can be found at the Web site for the National Institute for Health and Clinical Excellence (NICE): www.nice.org.uk/

- The Substance Abuse and Mental Health Services Administration (SAMHSA) has an initiative to evaluate, identify, and provide information on various mental health practices. Their work, entitled "The National Registry of Evidence-based Programs and Practices or NREPP," can be found online at www.nrepp.samhsa.gov

- The Agency for Health Care Policy and Research, now called the Agency for Healthcare Research and Quality (AHRQ), has established guidelines and criteria for identifying evidence-based practices and provides links to evidence-based clinical practice guidelines for various medical and mental health problems at www. ahrq. gov/clinic/epcix.htm

- The Cochrane Collaboration is an international network of professionals who conduct systematic reviews of research in human health care and health policy. Among their products are critical reviews of psychological treatment interventions and specific intervention questions. They can be found on the Web at www .cochrane.org

- Other reviews can be found in the reference section of Chapter 4 under "Empirical Support."

Chapter Review Test Questions

1. Which statement best describes the process used to identify ESTs?

   A. Consumers of mental health services nominated therapies.

   B. Experts came to a consensus based on their experiences with the treatments.

   C. Researchers submitted their works.

   D. Task groups reviewed the literature using clearly defined selection criteria for ESTs.

   Answer: D

2. Based on the differences in their criteria, in which of the following ways are *well-established* treatments different from those classified as *probably efficacious*?

   A. Only *probably efficacious* allowed the use of single-case design experiments.

   B. Only *well-established* allowed studies comparing the treatment to a psychological placebo.

   C. Only *well-established* required demonstration by at least two different, independent investigators or investigating teams.

   D. Only *well-established* allowed studies comparing the treatment to a pill placebo.

   Answer: C

Talking Points

Why would it be important to have a treatment effect demonstrated by at least two different investigators or investigating teams (i.e., independently replicated)?

- You can discuss sources of bias and confounds that may influence the outcome of a psychotherapy.

- In particular, consider discussing factors in some studies that can lead to *allegiance effects,* in which the positive outcome is found only by investigators who are, generally speaking, advocates of the therapy. Examples could include demand characteristics, advanced training in the techniques, and biased assessment of response.

Chapter References

Chambless, D. L., & Ollendick, T. H. (2001). Empirically supported psychological interventions: Controversies and evidence. *Annual Review of Psychology, 52,* 685–716.

Chambless, D. L., Sanderson, W. C., Shoham, V., Bennett Johnson, S., Pope, K. S., Crits-Christoph, P., . . . McCurry, S. (1996). An update on empirically validated therapies. *The Clinical Psychologist, 49,* 5–18.

Chambless, D. L., Baker, M. J., Baucom, D. H., Beutler, L. E., Calhoun, K. S., Crits-Christoph, P., . . . Woody, S. R. (1998). Update on empirically validated therapies, II. *The Clinical Psychologist, 51,* 3–16.

Gatz, M., Fiske, A., Fox, L. S., Kaskie, B., Kasl-Godley, J. E., McCallum, T., & Wetherell, J. (1998). Empirically validated psychological treatments for older adults. *Journal of Mental Health and Aging, 41,* 9–46.

Kendall, P. C., & Chambless, D. L. (Eds.). (1998). Empirically supported psychological therapies [special issue]. *Journal of Consulting and Clinical Psychology, 66*(3), 151–162.

Lonigan, C. J., & Elbert, J. C. (Eds.). (1998). Empirically supported psychosocial interventions for children [special issue]. *Journal of Clinical Child Psychology, 27,* 138–226.

Mitte, K. (2005). Meta-analysis of cognitive-behavioral treatments for generalized anxiety disorder: A comparison with pharmacotherapy. *Psychological Bulletin, 131,* 785–795.

Nathan, P. E., & Gorman, J. M. (Eds.). (1998). *A guide to treatments that work.* New York, NY: Oxford University Press.

Nathan, P. E., & Gorman, J. M. (Eds.). (2007). *A guide to treatments that work* (3rd ed.). New York, NY: Oxford University Press.

Spirito, A. (Ed.). (1999). Empirically supported treatments in pediatric psychology [special issue]. *Journal of Pediatric Psychology, 24,* 87–174.

What Are the Identified Empirically Supported Treatments for Generalized Anxiety Disorder?

Chapter Review

1. What types of treatment have been identified by reviewers and evidenced-based practice guidelines as efficacious for generalized anxiety disorder (GAD)?

Reviews Identifying CBT as an Evidence–Based Treatment for GAD

- American Psychological Association, Division 12: The Society of Clinical Psychology
- Barlow, Allen, & Basden (2007)
- Borkovec for Therapyadvisor.org
- Hunot et al. (2007) for Cochrane Database of Systematic Reviews
- The National Institute for Health and Clinical Excellence (NICE)
- International Consensus Group on Depression and Anxiety

---

2. What specific interventions are you likely to see in a more comprehensive cognitive behavioral therapy (CBT) for GAD?

Comprehensive CBT for GAD

- Self-monitoring of thoughts, feelings, and behaviors
- Relaxation training
  - Slowed, paced diaphragmatic breathing; progressive muscle relaxation
  - Meditation
  - Pleasant imagery
  - Applied relaxation
- Cognitive restructuring
  - Of automatic thoughts, images, and their underlying beliefs

(continued)

- Systematic graduated exposure
  - Imaginal, live, or both
- Stimulus control strategies
  - Worry time
- Behavioral strategies
  - Behavioral activation: Positive, pleasant, and/or self-worth-building activities that clients engage in on a daily basis
  - Problem-solving skills training

(Adapted, in part, from Borkovec in Therapyadvisor.org)

Key Points

- Treatments based on principles of cognitive behavioral therapy (CBT) are well-established as efficacious for GAD.
- The efficacy of applied relaxation and cognitive therapy has been highlighted by some reviewers and in some practice guidelines.
- More comprehensive CBT may also include exposure, stimulus control, and/or behavioral activation emphases.

Chapter Review Test Questions

1. Treatments based on the principles of which of the following therapeutic models have been identified by reviewers and evidence-based practice guideline developers (e.g., the National Institute for Health and Clinical Excellence) as having strong research support for the treatment of generalized anxiety disorder (GAD)?

   A. Cognitive-behavioral therapy

   B. Interpersonal therapy

   C. Psychoanalytic therapy

   D. Psychodynamic therapy

   Answer: A

2. As discussed in the chapter, the worry time intervention used in some forms of CBT for GAD is categorized under which of the following classes or types of interventions?

   A. Cognitive restructuring

   B. Problem solving

   C. Relaxation training

   D. Stimulus control

   Answer: D

──────── Talking Points ────────

As discussed in the chapter, applied relaxation has demonstrated efficacy in the treatment of generalized anxiety disorder, as has cognitive therapy. A point was made about how intervening in one domain (the physiological or cognitive) may also create change in another. Consider facilitating a discussion around examples of how this might occur. You could ask, for example, "How might reduction in the worry domain result in less physiological arousal?" The converse of this question could be asked, as well.

- Answers will reflect conceptualizations of the process. For example, one possible answer is that worry reflects an appraisal of threat. Appraisal of threat activates sympathetic arousal. Reducing the frequency, intensity, or duration of appraised threat is likely to reduce the sympathetic arousal that accompanies it. Encourage an open discussion of various interpretations.

Selected Chapter References

Reviews

Barlow, D. H., Allen, L. B., & Basden, S. L. (2007). Psychological treatments for panic disorders, phobias, and generalized anxiety disorder. In P. E. Nathan & J. M. Gorman's (Eds.), *A guide to treatments that work*. New York, NY: Oxford University Press.

Butler, A. C., Chapman, J. E., Forman, E. M., & Beck, A. T. (2006). The empirical status of cognitive-behavioral therapy: A review of meta-analyses. *Clinical Psychology Review, 26,* 17–31.

Gould, R. A., Safren, S. A., O'Neill Washington, D., & Otto, M. W. (2004). A meta-analytic review of cognitive-behavioral treatments. In R. G. Heimberg, C. L. Turk, and D. S. Mennin (Eds.), *Generalized anxiety disorder: Advances in research and practice* (pp. 248–264). New York, NY: Guilford Press.

Hunot, V., Churchill, R., Teixeira, V., & Silva de Lima, M. (2007). Psychological therapies for generalised anxiety disorder. *Cochrane Database of Systematic Reviews*, Issue 1. Art. No.: CD001848.

Mitte, K. (2005). Meta-analysis of cognitive-behavioral treatments for generalized anxiety disorder: A comparison with pharmacotherapy. *Psychological Bulletin, 131,* 785–795.

National Institute for Health and Clinical Excellence. (January 2011). *Anxiety: Clinical guideline CG113*. Available at http://guidance.nice.org.uk/CG113.

Empirical Support

Arntz, A. (2003). Cognitive therapy versus relaxation as treatment of generalized anxiety disorder. *Behaviour Research and Therapy, 41,* 633–646.

Barlow, D. H., Rapee, R. M., & Brown, T. A. (1992). Behavioral treatment of generalized anxiety disorder. *Behavior Therapy, 23,* 551–570.

Blowers, C., Cobb, J., & Mathews, A. (1987). Generalised anxiety: A controlled treatment study. *Behaviour Research and Therapy, 25,* 493–502.

Borkovec, T. D., & Costello, E. (1993). Efficacy of applied relaxation and cognitive-behavioral therapy in the treatment of generalized anxiety disorder. *Journal of Consulting and Clinical Psychology, 61,* 611–619.

Borkovec, T. D., Mathews, A. M., Chambers, A., Ebrahimi, S., Lytle, R., & Nelson, R. (1987). The effects of relaxation training with cognitive or nondirective therapy and the role of relaxation-induced anxiety in the treatment of generalized anxiety. *Journal of Consulting and Clinical Psychology, 55,* 883–933.

Borkovec, T. D., Newman, M. G., Pincus, A. L., & Lytle, R. (2002). A component analysis of cognitive-behavioral therapy for generalized anxiety disorder and the role of interpersonal problems. *Journal of Consulting and Clinical Psychology, 70,* 288–298.

Borkovec, T. D., & Ruscio, A. M. (2001). Psychotherapy for generalized anxiety disorder. *Journal of Clinical Psychiatry, 62,* 37–42.

Butler, G., Fennell, M., Robson, P., & Gelder, M. (1991). Comparison of behavior therapy and cognitive behavior therapy in the treatment of generalized anxiety disorder. *Journal of Consulting and Clinical Psychology, 59,* 167–175.

Dugas, M. J., Ladouceur, R., Leger, E., Freeston, M. H., Langlois, F., Provencher, M. D., & Boisvert, J. M. (2003). Group cognitive-behavioral therapy for generalized anxiety disorder: Treatment outcome and long-term follow-up. *Journal of Consulting and Clinical Psychology, 71*(4), 821–825.

Durham, R. C., Murphy, T., Allan, T., Richard, K., Treliving, L. R., & Fenton, G. W. (1994). Cognitive therapy, analytic psychotherapy and anxiety management training for generalised anxiety disorder. *The British Journal of Psychiatry, 165,* 315–323.

Kohli, A., Nehra, V., & Nehra, R. (2000). Comparison of efficacy of psychorelaxation and pharmacotherapy in generalized anxiety disorder. *Journal of Personality and Clinical Studies, 16,* 43–48.

Ladouceur, R., Dugas, M. J., Freeston, M. H., Léger, E., Gagnon, F., & Thibodeau, N. (2000). Efficacy of cognitive-behavioral treatment of generalized anxiety disorder: Evaluation in a controlled clinical trial. *Journal of Consulting and Clinical Psychology, 68,* 957–964.

Öst, L.-G., & Breitholtz, E. (2000). Applied relaxation vs. cognitive therapy in the treatment of generalized anxiety disorder. *Behaviour Research and Therapy, 38,* 777–790.

Power, K. G., Simpson, R. J., Swanson, V., & Wallace, L. A. (1990). A controlled comparison of cognitive-behaviour therapy, Diazepam, and placebo, alone and in combination, for the treatment of generalized anxiety disorder. *Journal of Anxiety Disorders, 4,* 267–292.

White, J., Keenan, M., & Brooks, N. (1992). Stress control: A controlled comparative investigation of large group therapy for generalized anxiety disorder. *Behavioural Psychotherapy, 20,* 97–114.

Clinical Resources

Beck, A. T., & Emery, G., with Greenberg, R. L. (1985). *Anxiety disorders and phobias: A cognitive perspective.* New York, NY: Basic Books.

Bernstein, D. A., & Borkovec, T. D. (1973). *Progressive relaxation training.* Champaign, IL: Research Press.

Brown, T. A., O'Leary, T., & Barlow, D. H. (2001). Generalized anxiety disorder. In D. H. Barlow (Ed.), *Clinical handbook of psychological disorders* (3rd ed., pp. 154–208). New York, NY: Guilford Press.

Dugas, M. J., & Robichaud, M. (2006). *Cognitive-behavioral treatment for generalized anxiety disorder: From science to practice.* New York, NY: Routledge.

Gorenstein, E. E., Papp, L. A., & Kleber, M. S. (1999). Cognitive-behavioral treatment of anxiety in later life. *Cognitive and Behavioral Practice, 6,* 305–319.

National Institute for Health and Clinical Excellence. (January 2011). Anxiety: Clinical guideline CG113. Available at http://guidance.nice.org.uk/CG113

Öst, L.-G. (1987). Applied relaxation: Description of a coping technique and review of controlled studies. *Behaviour Research and Therapy, 25,* 397–409.

Rygh, J., & Sanderson, W. C. (2004). *Treating generalized anxiety disorder.* New York, NY: Guilford Press.

White, J. (2008). *Overcoming generalized anxiety disorder: A relaxation, cognitive restructuring, and exposure-based protocol for the treatment of GA-therapist protocol.* Oakland, CA: New Harbinger.

Zinbarg, R. E., Craske, M. G., & Barlow, D. H. (2006). *Mastery of your anxiety and worry: Therapist guide* (2nd ed.). New York, NY: Oxford University Press.

Bibliotherapy Resources

Craske, M. G., & Barlow, D. H. (2006). *Mastery of your anxiety and worry: Client workbook* (2nd ed). New York, NY: Oxford University Press.

Leahy, R. (2006). *The worry cure: Seven steps to stop worry from stopping you.* New York, NY: Three Rivers Press.

Tompkins, M. A., & Martinez, K. A. (2009). *My anxious mind: A teen's guide to managing anxiety and panic.* Washington, DC: Magination Press.

White, J. (2008). *Overcoming generalized anxiety disorder: A relaxation, cognitive restructuring, and exposure-based protocol for the treatment of GAD-client manual.* Oakland, CA: New Harbinger.

5

How Do You Integrate Empirically Supported Treatments Into Treatment Planning?

This chapter is formatted differently from the others in this *Guide*. Rather than reviewing the *Chapter Review* questions and answers only, this chapter more closely follows the DVD and *Companion Workbook* to allow you to take participants through each step of the evidence-based treatment planning process.

This section of the DVD shows the viewer each step in the process of integrating ESTs into a treatment plan. It discusses each step of the treatment planning process for the identified problem (i.e., Behavioral Definitions, Goals, Objectives, and Treatment Interventions) and provides examples of how each can be written—with the objectives and interventions reflecting content consistent with the indicated EST. In this chapter, we have reproduced the examples of treatment plan statements shown on the DVD and included in the *Companion Workbook*. This gives you the option of stopping the DVD to discuss an example, or simply let it play.

For those interested in exploring issues related to the clinical delivery of the treatments discussed, vignettes are shown that demonstrate selected aspects of them. Each vignette is followed by a brief critique of the demonstration. The script of these vignettes, comments made in the critique, and a section allowing viewers to further critique are included in this *Guide* as well as the *Companion Workbook*. You can elect to facilitate this additional critique by viewers. Keep in mind that the vignettes demonstrate only selected aspects of the interventions discussed. They are informational in nature, to give the viewer an example of what a treatment might look like in its application, and are not intended to substitute for clinical training in the interventions discussed. Following selected vignettes, references may be made to homework assignments that can be found and reprinted at www.wiley.com/go/gadwb

These assignments also demonstrate selected therapeutic interventions consistent with those discussed in the DVD. These can also be reviewed and discussed at the facilitator's discretion.

Each section in this chapter is followed by section review questions, test-style questions, and an optional discussion question for use by the facilitator.

Integrating ESTs Into Treatment Planning

Construction of an empirically informed treatment plan for Generalized Anxiety Disorder (GAD) involves integrating objectives and treatment interventions consistent with identified empirically supported treatments (ESTs) into a client's treatment plan after you have determined that the client's primary problem fits those described in the target population of the EST research. Of course, implementing ESTs must be done in consideration of important client, therapist, and therapeutic relationship factors—consistent with the APA's definition of evidence-based practice.

Definitions

After determining that Generalized Anxiety Disorder is the primary presenting problem, we then add to the treatment plan those behavioral manifestations of GAD that define the client's expression of the disorder. Although there are commonalties in the presentation of GAD, the treatment plan is tailored to each client's particular expression of it.

Here is a list of behavioral definitions commonly used for GAD:

- Expresses excessive anxiety and worry that is difficult to control, occurring more days than not, for a period of at least six months, and is focused on several different events or activities.
- Displays restlessness or verbalizes feeling on edge.
- Reports feeling easily fatigued.
- Describes difficulty concentrating or mind going blank.
- Exhibits a general state of irritability.
- Displays and describes muscle tension.
- Reports an ongoing pattern of sleep disturbance (e.g., difficulty falling or staying asleep, or restless, unsatisfying sleep).

Note the focus on excessive anxiety and worry that define the disorder, and on the various manifestations of overarousal such as feeling on edge, having difficulty concentrating, and feeling generally irritable.

Goals

Goals are broad statements describing what you and the client would like the result of therapy to be. One statement may suffice, but more than one can be used in the treatment plan. Examples of common goal statements for GAD are the following:

- Reduce overall frequency, intensity, and duration of the anxiety so that daily functioning is not impaired.
- Stabilize anxiety level while increasing ability to function on a daily basis.
- Learn and implement coping skills that result in a reduction of anxiety and improved daily functioning.
- Resolve the core issue that is the source of anxiety.

Objectives and Interventions

We now direct our attention to client objectives and therapist interventions consistent with research-supported treatments for GAD. Objectives are statements that describe *small, observable steps the client must achieve* toward attaining the goal of successful treatment. Intervention statements describe the *actions taken by the therapist* to assist the client in achieving his/her objectives. Each objective must be paired with at least one intervention.

Assessment

Although common to all forms of therapy, the assessment phase of GAD treatment typically involves obtaining a detailed history, including the impact of the GAD on social, occupational, and interpersonal functioning. Psychological tests or objective measures may be used to supplement the clinical interview and/or track treatment response. A medical evaluation may be warranted to rule out medical or substance-related etiologies. A medication consultation may also be warranted if the client decides to explore this option. Table 5.1 contains examples of assessment objectives and interventions for GAD.

Table 5.1   Assessment Objectives and Interventions

Objectives	Interventions
1. Describe current and past experiences with the worry and anxiety symptoms, complete with their impact on functioning and attempts to resolve it.	1. Focus on developing a level of trust with the client; provide support and empathy to encourage the client to feel safe in expressing his/her GAD symptoms. 2. Ask the client to describe his/her past experiences of anxiety and their impact on functioning; assess the focus, excessiveness, and uncontrollability of the worry and the type, frequency, intensity, and duration of his/her anxiety symptoms (e.g., The Anxiety Disorders Interview Schedule for the DSM-IV by DiNardo, Brown, and Barlow).
2. Complete psychological tests designed to assess worry and anxiety symptoms.	1. Administer a self-report measure to help assess the nature and degree of the client's worry and anxiety symptoms (e.g., The Penn State Worry Questionnaire by Meyer, Miller, Metzger, and Borkovec) and the impact those symptoms have on functioning (e.g., OQ-45.2 by Lambert and Burlingame or the Symptom Checklist-90-R by Derogatis).
3. Complete a medical examination to assess for the possible contribution of medical or substance-related conditions to the anxiety.	1. Refer the client to a physician for a medical evaluation to rule out general medical or substance-related contributions to the GAD.
4. Cooperate with an evaluation by a prescribing practitioner for psychotropic medication.	1. Refer the client to a prescribing practitioner for a psychotropic medication consultation. 2. Monitor the client's psychotropic medication compliance, side effects, and effectiveness; confer regularly with the prescribing practitioner.

Psychoeducation

Empirically supported treatments for GAD emphasize initial and ongoing psychoeducation. In addition to helping facilitate a client's progress in therapy, the process and content of psychoeducation is used to reassure, instill hope, motivate, and otherwise enhance the therapeutic relationship. Common emphases of initial psychoeducation include conveying a conceptualization of GAD consistent with the treatment model, describing the treatment approach and its rationale, and enhancing engagement of the client in treatment. Reading or other educational material may also be assigned to supplement psychoeducation done within the session. Examples of an objective and interventions consistent with psychoeducation may look like these in Table 5.2.

Key Points

COMMON EMPHASES OF INITIAL PSYCHOEDUCATION INCLUDE:

1. Teaching the client about the nature and etiology of the diagnosed condition
2. Conveying a conceptualization of GAD consistent with the treatment model
3. Describing the treatment approach and explaining its rationale
4. Enhancing engagement of the client in treatment
5. Utilizing reading or other educational assignments as homework, if needed, to supplement psychoeducation done in session

---

Table 5.2   Assessment and Psychoeducation Objectives and Interventions

Objective	Interventions
5. Verbalize an understanding of the cognitive, physiological, and behavioral components of anxiety and its treatment.	1. Teach the client how generalized anxiety typically involves excessive worry about unrealistic threats, various bodily expressions of tension, overarousal, hypervigilance, and avoidance of what is threatening that interact to maintain the problem (see *Mastery of Your Anxiety and Worry—Therapist Guide* by Craske, Barlow, and O'Leary). 2. Discuss how treatment targets worry, anxiety symptoms, and avoidance to help the client manage worry effectively and reduce overarousal and unnecessary avoidance. 3. Assign the client to read psychoeducational sections of cognitive therapy books or treatment manuals on worry and generalized anxiety (e.g., *Mastery of Your Anxiety and Worry—Client Guide* by Zinbarg, Craske, Barlow, and O'Leary).

Assessment/Psychoeducation Review

1. What purposes can psychoeducation serve in therapy?

   In addition to helping facilitate a client's progress in therapy, the process and content of psychoeducation is used to reassure, instill hope, motivate, and otherwise enhance the therapeutic relationship.

2. What are common emphases of initial psychoeducation?

   Common emphases of initial psychoeducation include:

   ➤ Teaching the client about the nature and etiology of the diagnosed condition
   ➤ Conveying a conceptualization of GAD consistent with the treatment model
   ➤ Describing the treatment approach and explaining its rationale
   ➤ Enhancing engagement of the client in treatment
   ➤ Utilizing reading or other educational assignments as homework, if needed, to supplement psychoeducation done in session

---

Talking Points

As noted, psychoeducation is a process that permeates most psychotherapies. Consider facilitating a discussion of the various means through which psychoeducation might be conveyed. You might ask, "Through what various means might psychoeducational information be conveyed to a client?" You could also facilitate a discussion of how clients may have gained misinformation and its various sources.

Examples of common means through which psychoeducational information might be conveyed to the client include the following:

- Discussion with the therapist
- Reading of a pamphlet, fact sheet, chapter, or book
- Listening to a recording of information, exercise instructions, or a therapy session
- Attending a lecture

Assessment/Psychoeducation Review Test Question

1. At what point in therapy is psychoeducation conducted?

   A. At the end of therapy
   B. During the assessment phase
   C. During the initial treatment session
   D. Throughout therapy

   Correct: D

Cognitive–Behavioral Therapy: Relaxation Training

Let's move now to integrating objectives and interventions consistent with principles of CBT for GAD. As noted earlier, relaxation training is a staple of the CBT for GAD. To allow for flexibility of use and because clients may vary in which types of relaxation techniques they find effective, several methods of relaxation are often explored, including slowed, paced diaphragmatic breathing; progressive muscle relaxation; meditation; and pleasant imagery. As mentioned previously, therapists may also elect to use applied relaxation. Applied relaxation is a specific, stand-alone therapy in which the client progressively learns how to relax rapidly, and then uses this response in anxiety- or worry-provoking situations. A concurrent goal of all relaxation training is to help the client develop a more relaxed lifestyle—across all situations. Clients typically practice relaxation skills in session and through homework exercises toward the eventual objective of applying them in the context of their lives.

Relaxation training can be captured in an objective such as that used in number 6 in Table 5.3. Treatment interventions for relaxation training should capture the type of relaxation training that will be taught, including homework assignments related to practicing the relaxation skill. As always, reading assignments or other educational interventions may be made to supplement interventions initiated in session.

Key Points

- Several approaches to relaxation training could be incorporated into the treatment plan, including slowed, paced diaphragmatic breathing; progressive muscle relaxation; meditation; pleasant imagery; and applied relaxation.
- Relaxation is typically taught in session, and then practiced by the client outside of therapy.
- Reading or other forms of teaching the techniques (e.g., CDs, DVDs) may be used to supplement training.

Table 5.3   Relaxation Training Objectives and Interventions

Objective	Interventions
6. Learn and implement calming skills to reduce overall anxiety and manage anxiety symptoms.	1. Teach the client relaxation skills (e.g., progressive muscle relaxation, imagery, diaphragmatic breathing, verbal cues for deep relaxation), how to discriminate better between relaxation and tension, as well as how to apply these skills to his/her daily life (e.g., see *Progressive Relaxation Training* by Bernstein and Borkovec; *Treating GAD* by Rygh and Sanderson). 2. Assign the client homework each session in which he or she practices relaxation exercises daily for at least 15 minutes; review the exercises, reinforcing success while providing corrective feedback toward improvement. 3. Assign the client to read about progressive muscle relaxation and other calming strategies in relevant books or treatment manuals (e.g., *Progressive Relaxation Training* by Bernstein and Borkovec; *Mastery of Your Anxiety and Worry—Client Guide* by Zinbarg, Craske, Barlow, and O'Leary).

Table 5.3 gives examples of an objective and interventions for Relaxation Training for the treatment of GAD.

Demonstration Vignette
Relaxation Training

Here we present the transcript of the dialogue depicted in the Relaxation Training vignette.

Therapist: Over the last number of sessions, Jan, we've been focusing on you learning the deep-muscle, deep-breathing relaxation technique. We started with you systematically tensing and then relaxing small groups of muscles throughout your body until you were completely and deeply relaxed. Then we grouped muscles together and asked you to tense and relax these larger groups, such as both of your hands, arms, and shoulders at one time. This is intended to make the relaxation technique shorter while still being effective. Then we did the release-only technique, leaving the tension phase out. This, too, reduces the time it takes to relax. Has it done that?

Client: Yeah, I was able to relax more quickly using the release-only approach.

Therapist: Perfect. Today we're going to take this relaxation skill you're learning a step further. We're going to first have you relax using the release-only technique. When you get completely relaxed, I'll ask you to pair the relaxed state with the cue words you chose: "Be calm." While you are relaxed, I will ask you to take a deep breath. As you exhale, I want you to say the words "be calm," and release tension as you are saying them. Do you follow me?

Client: I think so. After I am relaxed, I take a deep breath, and say the words "be calm" to myself as I exhale, right?

Therapist: Exactly. Then you will breathe normally, scan your body for tension, then again take a deep breath, exhale, and say "be calm." Then we're just going to repeat that awhile. I'll guide you through the procedure just like we've done before. Any questions?

Client: No, I'm ready.

Therapist: Okay. Why don't you lay back, close your eyes, and stretch out in the recliner, allowing your entire body to be supported and comfortable. [patient reclines] Now, take a slow, deep breath and then exhale slowly, releasing tension as you breathe out.

Next, please focus on the first muscle group of both hands, both arms, and shoulders. Take a deep breath [client does], now exhale and release tension [client does], and feel the heaviness as the tension leaves. Relax these muscles and feel the blood rush in to provide warmth. Notice how it feels to be warm and relaxed while you breathe deeply and smoothly. . . .

Fade out.

Fade in.

Great, Jan. Now that we've gone through all the muscle groups, please rate your relaxation for me on a scale of one to ten, with ten being the deepest possible relaxed state.

Client: I'm about an eight.

Therapist: Wonderful. Good job. Now, stay warm and relaxed [pause]. Now, breathe deeply, exhale, and say the words "be calm" to yourself. (Give these directions slowly with proper pauses.) Allow the words "be calm" to produce even deeper relaxation. Now, breathe in slowly and deeply, breathe out slowly and say "be calm" to yourself. Good. Let's do it again. Breathe in deeply and now breathe out saying "be calm" gently in your mind. Very good.

Now open your eyes slowly as I count to five: one, two, three, four, five. Good. You're alert again. How do you feel, Jan?

Client: Great. It's so good to just let loose of all the tension I carry around. [client sits up]

Therapist: Excellent. This is a skill that we are going to use in various situations, some of which have triggered anxiety and muscle tension. So let's see if we can start putting together a list of possible situations. What situations come to mind?

Client: Well, I don't know. I get tense while I'm driving, especially on the expressway. And whenever I'm around my supervisor at work, I'm all nerves.

Therapist: Uh-huh. Those are two excellent examples of situations in which you could repeat the cue words to yourself, breathe deeply, and prompt the relaxation response. Let's look for some more . . .

Critique of the Relaxation Training Demonstration Vignette

The following points were made in the critique:

a. Therapist gives a good summary of previous sessions' work and then gives an "advanced organizer" to client for what will be the focus of current session.

b. A reclined position is helpful in achieving a relaxed state.

c. Therapist's use of rating scale is helpful for tracking client's progress and quantifying the relaxation results.

d. Use of the cue word paired with the relaxed state (i.e., cue controlled relaxation) is an application of classical conditioning.

e. Client's affirmation of being "relaxed and alert" is important as it is in contrast to an anxious client's common state of being alert and tense.

f. Specifying how the behavioral coping skill will be applied to everyday life situations of the client is critical.

Additional points that could be made:

a. This session can only be held after the client is taught the relaxation skill in more detail, one muscle group at a time in earlier sessions.

b. The therapist must be careful not to rush the relaxation process; use pauses and talk slowly as the process is proceeding.

Comments you would like to make:

____

____

____

____

Homework: The homework exercise "Safe and Peaceful Place Meditation" (*Veterans and Active Duty Military Psychotherapy Homework Planner* by Finley & Moore) is another example of an activity that is useful for managing stress and anxiety. It guides the client in a personalized multisensory imagery exercise in which he or she creates a mental construct of a safe and peaceful place and practices temporarily withdrawing from engagement with stressors. Cue words are also used in this exercise to trigger the relaxation state (see www.wiley.com/go/gadwb). Other resources for homework assignments for relaxation are *Progressive Relaxation Training* by Bernstein and Borkovec, and *Mastery of Your Anxiety and Worry—Client Guide* by Zinbarg, Craske, Barlow, and O'Leary.

Relaxation Training Review

1. What types of techniques might be used by the client to help induce relaxation?

   Examples of techniques that might be used by the client to help induce relaxation include, but are not limited to, slowed, paced diaphragmatic breathing; progressive muscle relaxation; meditation; and pleasant imagery. Applied relaxation is a specific therapy in which the client progressively learns how to relax rapidly and then uses this response in the context of his/her life.

2. Toward what objectives is relaxation training done?

   Relaxation skills are often taught as a coping strategy for use before, during, and after any anticipated stressful events. They are also taught to help the client develop a more relaxed lifestyle by frequently inducing the relaxed state throughout the day.

——— Talking Points ———

- As noted, one of the objectives of relaxation training is to help the client develop a more relaxed approach to day-to-day life. For the client, this usually begins by learning the relaxation skill and then applying it in various situations—stressful and not. Consider facilitating a brainstorming session of various ways a client might approach accomplishing this broader objective of a more relaxed lifestyle.

- Considerations include integrating physical relaxation into various activities as described previously, including pairing repeated daily activities with relaxation (e.g., driving, sitting at a desk, talking on the phone). Some cognitive interventions may help the client take a more flexible, adaptive approach to activities. Integrating relaxing, pleasurable activities into one's schedule is another commonly used technique. You could also introduce the importance of having a flexible repertoire of skills that facilitate one's adaptation to life demands. In this case, the question "Why would it be important for clients to have more than one way of relaxing?" might prompt this discussion.

Relaxation Training Review Test Question

1. As discussed in the chapter, what is the rationale for having a therapist consider teaching various methods of relaxation to a client as opposed to just one?

   A. Because all types of relaxation techniques have demonstrated efficacy in the treatment of GAD.

   B. Because it allows for flexibility of use and because clients may vary in which types of relaxation techniques they find effective.

   C. Because using multiple types of relaxation relaxes the client more than using one.

   D. Because using one type of relaxation does not relax the client as well as using many.

   Answer: B

Cognitive-Behavioral Therapy: Stimulus Control/Worry Time

Stimulus control techniques, such as establishing a worry time, are behavioral interventions that have been used in some applications of CBT for GAD. The rationale for their use is that worry is paired with environmental contexts or stimuli, and therefore is under poor stimulus control (i.e., it can be triggered by multiple environmental stimuli). Although clients with GAD may find it difficult to simply stop worrying, they may be able to develop the skill of postponing it, thus bringing it under better stimulus control and having an opportunity to better address it.

The technique involves establishing a worry time and place in which clients address daily worries specifically. They learn to identify worries as soon as they begin and postpone them to the worry time. They do this by using appropriate cognitive coping strategies such as self-talk, which is designed to delay engagement in the worry and redirect attentional focus back to the task at hand. They repeat this process each time a worry is detected. Once the worry time is reached, it is used to address worries using techniques acquired through the therapy, such as problem solving.

As reflected in objective number 7 and its treatment interventions, stimulus control can be incorporated into your treatment plan through interventions that capture the rationale and major features of the technique. These include limiting the associations between environmental stimuli and worry by restricting worry to a specific time and place. This also requires the client to develop the skill of identifying, stopping, and delaying worry until the worry time.

Key Points

- Worry occurs in many environmental contexts and therefore is under poor stimulus control.
- Clients are taught the skill of postponing worry to a specific time and place, thus bringing it under better stimulus control and having an opportunity to better address it.
- Clients learn to identify worries and postpone them until the worry time.
- Once the worry time is reached, it is used to address worries using techniques acquired through the therapy, such as problem solving.

Table 5.4 contains examples of an objective and interventions consistent with stimulus control/worry time for GAD.

Table 5.4   Stimulus Control/Worry Time Objectives and Interventions

Objective	Interventions
7. Learn and implement a strategy to limit the association between various environmental settings and worry, delaying the worry until a designated worry time.	1. Explain the rationale for using a worry time as well as how it is to be used; agree upon a worry time and place with the client and implement it. 2. Teach the client how to recognize, stop, and delay worry until the agreed-upon worry time using skills such as thought stopping and relaxation.

Demonstration Vignette
Stimulus Control/Worry Time

Here we present the transcript of the dialogue depicted in the Stimulus Control/Worry Time therapy vignette.

Therapist: Thanks, Jan, for completing this log of the worries you've had between our sessions. Why don't we take a look at it? You know how we've talked about how all worries are anticipations of things to come?

Client: Yeah.

Therapist: Well, it seems a lot of yours are focused on the very next thing you're about to do in your day.

Client: They are?

Therapist: Yeah, let me read them to you. Getting the kids off to school on time, what to make them for lunch, whether it's nutritional enough, getting ready for work, the traffic you'll face going to work, whether you'll get your work done, whether you get in trouble with your supervisor, how much homework the kids have. It kind of follows your day.

Client: That's true. I pretty much worry about everything that's coming up.

Therapist: It looks like it. And because your worries anticipate routine events in your day, they occur in various situations, at various times, and repeat themselves day after day.

Client: It does feel like it never really stops.

Therapist: I'm sure it does. One thing that's important for us to see is that when we worry in several settings or situations repeatedly, just returning to that situation can trigger our worries again. They get associated. And repeating them keeps that setting and worry association alive.

Client: Just being in that situation triggers the worry?

Therapist: Yeah. Take making lunch, for instance. You get yourself in that setting and start looking for what to make, and what worry pops up in your head?

Client: Lots. Like what should I make? Do I have time? Is it nutritious? Will it spoil? You name it.

Therapist: Exactly. Did you plan to worry about these things, or do they just seem to come up?

(continued)

Client: They just come up. I mean, I have to do these things. I can't not do them.

Therapist: That's true, but because we know that these settings are capable of triggering the worry, what we can work with is how you respond to the worry that's triggered.

Client: How?

Therapist: Well, first, the worries are going to come. It's your reaction to the situation. But let's make a distinction between your worry reaction and your response to that reaction. So let's say that your reaction to the situation is a worry. What's your response to that worry typically been?

Client: I'm not sure. I guess I just try to prevent whatever I'm worrying about from happening.

Therapist: Okay. So in a sense you stay focused on the worry and focused on trying to prevent it?

Client: Yeah.

Therapist: So the situation and the worry get associated more. What other responses could you have besides that one; maybe one that reduces that association?

Client: I don't know.

Therapist: Well, let's look at options. One could be to respond to it by letting the worry go. But you usually don't let it go?

Client: No, not at all. I just get caught up in it. I can't help it.

Therapist: I understand. Worry makes us feel threatened, and we have a tendency to stay focused on what we find threatening. But we're not cemented into that response. We can try different ones and see their effect on us.

Client: Like what?

Therapist: Well, our goal here is to try to disconnect worry from these situations. But the worry is going to happen. At this stage of the therapy, are you willing to just try to move those worries, put them off, postpone them to a single time and setting where you can worry about them there and then? It's called worry time.

Client: Boy, I don't know if I can do that.

Therapist: I understand. Do you see how your reaction, right now, to my suggestion to move the worries to a worry time, is to worry about whether you can do it?

Client: Yeah, I guess I am.

Therapist: Okay, so let's try this with that worry right now. Are you willing to give it a shot?

Client: Yeah, I'll try it. But how?

Therapist: Let's talk about that. This is a new way of responding to your worry at the moment you notice it's happening. Our goal is to postpone them until your worry time. Our plan is to build on some of the things you're already doing, like monitoring your worry, using your relaxation skill, and add a few mental skills intended to stop a worrisome train of thought and redirect your focus.

Client: All right. I'd like to learn that.

Therapist: Good.

Critique of the Stimulus Control/Worry Time Demonstration Vignette

The following points were made in the critique:

a. Good use of homework and integrating it into the session.

b. Therapist uses sound empathy skills, emphasizing the necessity for relationship skills while applying any therapeutic technique.

c. Therapist engages the client in the process of seeing how concepts can be applied to her daily life; he does not just lecture to her.

d. Therapist differentiates between patient's worry reaction and her response to it. This is a step toward getting her to take control of her response to worry and postpone it until the agreed-upon worry time and place.

e. Therapist is using various CBT techniques, such as relaxation, stimulus control, and thought stopping; he integrates them for the client at the end of the session.

Additional points that could be made:

a. This technique could more accurately be called "Worry Time and Place" because the client will be encouraged to delay addressing the worry until an agreed-upon time and place in an attempt to break the association between the current environmental stimuli and the worry reaction.

b. Therapist tries to engage the client in the problem-solving process by considering alternative options to her reaction to the worry.

c. Client will be asked to address her worry for a specified time of, say, 15 minutes at 8:00 p.m. and perhaps in a place like her recliner.

Comments you would like to make:

____

____

____

____

     Homework: No specific homework exercises for Worry Time are currently available in the Practice*Planner* series, but a resource for the client that includes this technique, *The Worry Cure: Seven Steps to Stop Worry from Stopping You* by Robert Leahy, the reference to which can be found in Chapter 4 of this workbook.

Stimulus Control/Worry Time Review

1. What is the rationale for using a worry time?

   The rationale for its use is that worry occurs in many environmental contexts and therefore is under poor stimulus control—because it can be prompted across several environments. Developing the skill of postponing it until a worry time and place brings it under better stimulus control and gives clients an opportunity to better address it.

2. What is the worry time technique?

The technique involves establishing a worry time and place in which clients address daily worries specifically. They learn to identify worries as soon as they begin and postpone them until the worry time using appropriate cognitive coping strategies such as self-talk, which is designed to delay engagement in the worry and to redirect attentional focus to the task at hand. They repeat this process each time a worry is detected. Once the worry time is reached, it is used to address worries using techniques acquired through the therapy, such as problem solving or exposure.

Talking Points

Using the worry time technique requires clients to be able to know when they are worrying and then postpone the worry to the selected time and place. Consider facilitating a discussion around teaching clients how to know when they are worrying. You might ask, "How would you go about helping your client learn the skill of knowing when they are worrying and doing something about it?" Some options to consider, from cognitive therapy, include the following:

- Providing psychoeducation about the connection between thought and feeling.
- Teaching the client to pay attention to the feelings that typically accompany worrisome thought; that is, using the feelings as the indicator that worrisome thought is occurring.
- Teaching the client key words in self-talk that are indicative of worry (e.g., "What if . . .").
- Having the client self-monitor and record the worry process.
- Reading about common worries and how they sound in one's head.

Stimulus Control/Worry Time Review Test Question

1. Which of the following statements best describes an objective of the worry time procedure?

    A. To have a common language between the therapist and client: When one is worrying, both call that the worry time

   B. To postpone worries to a specific time and place where they can be addressed productively

   C. To recognize that whenever one is worrying, it is time to address it productively

   D. To recognize that whenever one is worrying, the environmental stimulus causing it needs to be identified

Answer: B

Cognitive–Behavioral Therapy: Cognitive Restructuring

Cognitive theory holds that the anxiety and worrying in GAD stem from biased, maladaptive ways of perceiving and interpreting the world. Standard cognitive therapy techniques are used for addressing these biases. They include learning the connections among thoughts, feelings, and actions; identifying relevant automatic thoughts, images, and their underlying beliefs; challenging the biases; developing alternative perspectives; and testing biased and alternative beliefs through behavioral experiments.

Objectives and therapeutic interventions descriptive of the cognitive restructuring component of CBT for GAD highlight the major features of the cognitive therapy process. Homework assignments related to any of these tasks are used commonly in the therapy.

Key Points

- Cognitive theory holds that the anxiety and worrying in GAD stem from biased, maladaptive ways of perceiving and interpreting the world.
- Standard cognitive therapy techniques include the following:
  - Learning the connections among thoughts, feelings, and actions
  - Identifying relevant automatic thoughts, images, and their underlying beliefs
  - Challenging the biases
  - Developing alternative perspectives
  - Testing biased and alternative beliefs through behavioral experiments

---

Table 5.5 contains examples of objectives and interventions consistent with Cognitive Restructuring for GAD.

Table 5.5   Cognitive Restructuring Objectives and Interventions

Objectives	Interventions
8. Verbalize an understanding of the role that cognitive biases play in excessive irrational worry and persistent anxiety symptoms.	1. Discuss examples demonstrating how unrealistic worry typically overestimates the probability of threats and underestimates or overlooks the client's ability to manage realistic demands and uncertainty (or assign "Past Successful Anxiety Coping" in the *Adult Psychotherapy Homework Planner*, 2nd ed., by Jongsma). 2. Assist the client in analyzing his/her fear by examining the probability of the negative expectation occurring, the real consequences of it occurring, his/her ability to control the outcome, the worst possible outcome, and his/her ability to accept it (see "Analyze the Probability of a Feared Event" in *Adult Psychotherapy Homework Planner*, 2nd ed., by Jongsma, and *Anxiety Disorders and Phobias* by Beck and Emery).
9. Identify, challenge, and replace biased, worrisome self-talk and beliefs with positive, realistic, and empowering self-talk.	1. Explore the client's biased schema and self-talk that mediate his/her fear response; assist him/her in generating thoughts that correct for the biases; use behavioral experiments to test fearful versus alternative predictions. 2. Assign the client a homework exercise in which he or she identifies fearful self-talk, identifies biases in the self-talk, generates alternatives, and tests through behavioral experiments; review and reinforce success, providing corrective feedback toward improvement.

Demonstration Vignette
Cognitive Restructuring

Here we present the transcript of the dialogue depicted in the Cognitive Restructuring therapy vignette.

Therapist: Jan, we talked last session about starting to use this form to help guide you through the process of evaluating your worries. Why don't we go through it with one of the worries that you've identified to give you a sense for how to use it between our sessions. Sound okay?

Client: Yeah, I want to be able to understand this.

Therapist: Okay, well, our first step is to select a specific worry. As a starter, how about working with the worry that you won't be able to get the kids' lunches made?

Client: Sure, that's a daily thing.

Therapist: So the first question we want to ask has to do with the fact that all worries are anticipations. Remember that idea?

Client: Yeah, I understand that. They're all about what *could* happen.

Therapist: Exactly. So what we're going to do is turn that anticipation into a prediction. That is, we're going to make the worry make a prediction of what it says is going to happen. So specifically, what is the worry predicting will happen here with the lunches?

Client: That I won't get the lunches made—that the kids will go to school without a lunch.

Therapist: Excellent, that's exactly what it's saying. Next question, how likely is this to actually happen? Zero to 100 percent. Zero means it's not going to happen, 100 means it's definitely going to happen, 50 means a 50-50 chance.

Client: I don't know. I guess, 20 percent, maybe.

Therapist: Okay. Now, how bad would it be if it actually occurred, 0 to 100, with 100 being the absolute worst?

Client: Oh . . . an 80, maybe an 80? It wouldn't be good at all.

Therapist: Okay, now since you're estimating that there's only a 20% chance of it happening, the next question is "What is the most likely thing to happen?"

Client: Well, that I get the lunches made, I guess.

Therapist: Right, so that's what's most likely. Now, next question, what is the worst thing that could happen if you don't get the kids' lunches made?

Client: The kids will starve, I guess.

Therapist: Starve?

Client: I guess be hungry is more accurate.

Therapist: It is. So they would be hungry. And then what would happen?

Client: I don't know, maybe they won't be able to concentrate at school. I don't know.

Client: I guess I would feel bad. That's probably the worst thing, I guess. I never really thought about this.

Therapist: Right, that's exactly why we're doing it. So let's stay with it a little longer. [nods approval]. Okay, a little switch here: So what's the best outcome here, even if you don't get the lunches made?

Client: I don't know . . . maybe they could get lunch at school.

Therapist: Okay, good.

Client: I've never stopped to think like this.

(continued)

Therapist: That's exactly what this form helps you do. So, let's go to the next section. It's an important one. I think you're already doing this in your head, but let's do it this way for now. We're going to look at the evidence in your life and see if it supports the prediction that the worry is making, or if it supports something other than the worry. Let's start with the likelihood question. You said there was a 20% chance of not getting the lunch made. So, in the past, how many times have the kids gone to school without lunch?

Client: Well, actually none.

Therapist: Never?

Client: No, I've always made them.

Therapist: Okay, so one thing we can see with this process is that the worry way overestimates the actual likelihood of what it's worrying about.

Client: Well, I'm not sure what you mean.

Therapist: Let me ask another way. How many times have you had this particular worry?

Client: Oh, hundreds, probably thousands. I don't know, a lot.

Therapist: Okay. So if we could have gone back in time and made this worry make this prediction each time it was there, how many times would it have been right?

Client: Um, never.

Therapist: Never. Not once. And how many times has it been wrong?

Client: I see, thousands.

Therapist: Right. So Jan, if this worry was a real person who was telling you every morning, "You're not going to be able to get the lunch made," and every single time it was wrong, what do you think you might tell this person after a while?

Client: To shut up, I suppose.

Therapist Yeah, who wouldn't? Let me ask you, do you ever talk to your worry that way—like you would if it was a person constantly telling you that bad things are going to happen, even though they never actually do happen?

Client: No, I never do. I don't like that the worry is there, but I never thought of telling it off.

Critique of the Cognitive Restructuring Demonstration Vignette

The following points were made in the critique:

   a. This is a formal approach to teaching the cognitive restructuring technique through the use of a form that asks specific questions.

   b. The client's probability biases are examined to help her see that they overestimate the likelihood and severity of a bad outcome.

   c. Client acknowledges that she does not typically examine her fears, but rather just accepts them and reacts to them as if they are reasonable.

d. Therapist leads the client to the conclusion that she overestimates the probability of a negative outcome by looking at the actual outcome of past worry predictions.

e. The therapist encourages the client to use self-talk to challenge her fears with an unbiased alternative.

Additional points that could be made:

a. Instead of just selecting a generic example of a worry to teach the technique of examining biases, the therapist selects one from the client's daily life, making the process more relevant and applicable.

Comments you would like to make:

____

____

____

____

Homework: The exercise "Analyze the Probability of a Feared Event" (*Adult Psychotherapy Homework Planner*, 2nd ed., by Jongsma) leads the client to identify the distorted cognitions that feed the fear and suggest realistic, positive self-talk to counteract this strong mediation effect. Other homework exercises that focus on changing the thoughts that trigger negative emotions are "Journal and Replace Self-Defeating Thoughts," "Negative Thoughts Trigger Negative Feelings," and "Journal of Distorted, Negative Thoughts" (see www.wiley.com/go/gadwb).

Cognitive Restructuring Review

1. In brief, what is the cognitive theory of GAD?

   Cognitive theory holds that the anxiety and worrying in GAD stem from biased, maladaptive ways of perceiving and interpreting the world. Common biases include overestimating threat, underestimating self-efficacy in managing outcomes, and needing certainty regarding future events.

2. What techniques are standard to cognitive therapy?

   Techniques used for addressing biased cognition include learning the connections among thoughts, feelings, and actions; identifying relevant automatic thoughts, images, and their underlying beliefs; challenging the biases by first treating them as hypotheses rather than as facts and then subjecting them to logical and empirical analysis, developing alternative perspectives for which there is evidence, and testing biased and alternative beliefs through behavioral experiments.

——— Talking Points ———

Cognitive biases maintaining GAD often overestimate the likelihood and severity of feared events. Consider facilitating a discussion of common worries in GAD and how they reflect this bias.

COMMON EXAMPLES OF ADULT WORRIES INCLUDE:
- Daily responsibilities
- Health of family members
- Safety of children
- Finances
- Job security
- Relationships

THEME OF CHILDHOOD WORRIES IN GAD:
- Quality or competence of behavioral performance at home or in school

You may want to expand the discussion to include implicit themes of these biases, such as underestimating competency (e.g., worrisome thought assumes that the worrier will not know how to handle X or will handle it badly), demands for perfectionism/dichotomous thinking (e.g., that things must go perfectly or they are bad), and demands for certainty (e.g., that certainty about future events is necessary before one can stop worrying), among others.

Cognitive Restructuring Review Test Question

1. Through discussions with her therapist, Jan comes to understand that her anxious feelings escalate when she is thinking worrisome thoughts about not getting her children's lunches made on time. This represents what process in cognitive therapy?

    A. Identifying the connection between thought and emotion
    B. Identifying the biases contained in self-talk
    C. Monitoring self-talk
    D. Shifting from biased to alternative beliefs and predictions
    Answer: A

Cognitive–Behavioral Therapy: Exposure Therapy

Let's move on now to examples of objectives and interventions that are consistent with the exposure therapy component of CBT for GAD. Although it is not characteristic of patients with GAD to have phobic-like fears of specific objects or situations, feared and avoided situations may be evident with some clients. When this is the case, systematic graduated exposure techniques (imaginal and/or in vivo) may be implemented. A common application is to assign homework in which the patient deliberately approaches feared or worry-eliciting situations while deploying one's newly developed cognitive and relaxation coping strategies. Because the worry process in GAD can become so habitual, a form of imaginal exposure such as self-control desensitization may be used. In self-control desensitization, clients repeatedly imagine anxiety-provoking or worrisome situations while imagining themselves coping successfully by using relaxation and other newly learned skills.

Key Points

- Feared and avoided situations may be present in GAD.
- When this is evident, systematic graduated exposure techniques (imaginal and/or in vivo) may be implemented.
- In exposure in vivo, clients deliberately approach feared or worry-eliciting situations while deploying their newly developed cognitive and relaxation coping strategies.
- Self-control desensitization, in which the clients repeatedly imagine anxiety-provoking or worrisome situations while imagining themselves coping successfully, may also be used.

Table 5.6 contains examples of an objective and interventions consistent with Exposure Therapy for GAD.

Table 5.6   Exposure Therapy Objectives and Interventions

Objectives	Interventions
10. Deliberately imagine and/or actually approach worry-eliciting situations while using newly learned coping strategies.	1. Conduct systematic graduated exposure to worry-provoking situations in which the client uses newly learned coping skills. 2. Assign the client homework exercises in which they practice self-control desensitization, graduated exposure, or both; record and review in subsequent session toward the goal of mastery. 3. Conduct self-control desensitization in which the client imagines worry-provoking situations and imagines coping with them successfully by using relaxation, cognitive, problem-solving, and/or other skills learned in therapy.

Exposure Therapy Review

1. When might exposure be incorporated into the treatment plan for GAD?

   Although it is not characteristic of patients with GAD to have phobic-like fears of specific objects or situations, feared and avoided situations may be evident with some clients. When this is the case, systematic graduated exposure techniques (imaginal and/or in vivo) may be implemented.

2. What types of exposure are commonly used for GAD?

   Exposure in vivo: A common application exposure is to assign homework in which clients deliberately approach feared or worry-eliciting situations while deploying their newly developed cognitive and relaxation coping strategies.

   Imaginal exposure such as self-control desensitization: In self-control desensitization, clients repeatedly imagine anxiety-provoking or worrisome situations while imagining themselves coping successfully by using relaxation and other newly learned skills.

Talking Points

Consider facilitating a discussion about how exposure produces beneficial change for the client. Participants' conceptualizations of its mechanism(s) of action will influence their answers and, hopefully, serve as the basis of a good discussion. This topic can be prompted by asking the question directly, or with an indirect one such as this: "What do you think clients experience/learn through the course of exposure therapy that reduces their worries and avoidance of these situations?"

EXAMPLES OF WHAT MAY BE LEARNED INCLUDE:
- Skills for managing the demands they fear
- Confidence and a sense of self-efficacy in managing situations
- Validation of alternative predictions that facilitate a shift in belief from threatening to more reassuring appraisals of the situation and one's capacity to manage them
- The extinction of conditioned anxiety
- Others

Exposure Therapy Review Test Question

1. One form of exposure that may be used in the treatment of generalized anxiety disorder is self-control desensitization. Which of the following best describes this procedure?

   A. Clients deliberately approach actual anxiety-provoking or worrisome situations while using skills learned in therapy to manage their reaction.

   B. Clients repeatedly imagine anxiety-provoking or worrisome situations while imagining themselves coping successfully by using relaxation and other newly learned skills.

   C. Clients repeatedly pair a relaxing word with a state of relaxation.

   D. Clients learn how to relax rapidly and then apply this skill in various actual anxiety-provoking or worrisome situations.

Answer: B

Cognitive–Behavioral Therapy: Behavioral Strategies

Lastly, many CBT approaches employ other behavioral strategies, such as behavioral activation and problem-solving skills training, when treating GAD. In behavioral activation, clients are encouraged to identify pleasant, worthwhile, or self-concept-building activities that they can engage in on a daily basis. Such activities create pleasant circumstances for focused attention, build self-esteem, and generate positive affect counter to the anxious and depressed moods that often accompany worry.

Problem-solving skills training is a common behavioral intervention used in CBT for many disorders. It teaches an orientation to problems that accepts that they will occur, as well as a systematic approach for addressing them. The primary steps involved in problem solving are as follows:

1. Define the problem specifically.
2. Generate options for addressing the problem.
3. Evaluate the pros and cons of the generated solution options.
4. Select the best solution and implement it.
5. Evaluate the effectiveness of the plan.
6. Keep, revise, or change the plan based on the evaluation of its effectiveness.

Problem solving guides clients to address worries productively and counters the more ruminative habit characteristic of GAD. Homework assignments in which problem solving is implemented, recorded, and reviewed are commonly used.

Table 5.7 contains examples of objectives and interventions consistent with Behavioral Strategies for GAD.

Key Points

- Many CBT approaches employ other behavioral strategies in treating GAD.

- Behavioral activation and problem-solving skills are common examples.

- Behavioral activation encourages engagement in pleasant, worthwhile, or self-concept-building activities.

- Problem-solving skills training teaches an orientation to problems that accepts that they will occur, as well as systematic steps for addressing them.

- Problem solving guides clients to address worries productively.

- Homework assignments in which behavioral strategies are implemented, recorded, and reviewed are commonly used.

Table 5.7   Behavioral Strategies Objectives and Interventions

Objectives	Interventions
11. Identify and engage in pleasant activities on a daily basis.	1. Engage the client in behavioral activation, increasing the client's contact with sources of reward, identifying processes that inhibit activation, and teaching skills to solve life problems; use behavioral techniques such as instruction, rehearsal, role-playing, and role reversal as needed, to assist adoption in the client's daily life; reinforce success.
12. Learn and implement problem-solving strategies for realistically addressing worries.	1. Teach the clients problem-solving strategies in which they take a positive problem orientation and utilize problem-solving steps to address problems, including defining and pinpointing the problem, developing a list of possible solutions, analyzing and comparing the pros and cons of each solution, selecting and implementing a solution, analyzing the solution for effectiveness, and adjusting the action if necessary for mutual satisfaction. 2. Assign the client a homework exercise in which he or she implements problem-solving skills for a current problem (see "Applying Problem-Solving to Interpersonal Conflict" in *Adult Psychotherapy Homework Planner*, 2nd ed., by Jongsma; *Mastery of Your Anxiety and Worry—Client Guide* by Zinbarg, Craske, Barlow, and O'Leary; or *Generalized Anxiety Disorder* by Brown, O'Leary, and Barlow); review, reinforcing success and providing corrective feedback toward improvement.

Demonstration Vignette

Behavioral Strategies: Problem-Solving Therapy

Here we present the transcript of the dialogue depicted in Behavioral Strategies: Problem-Solving Therapy vignette.

Therapist: Jan, in our session last week we began to apply problem solving to an issue that has made you anxious. We worked first at pinpointing the problem in specific terms and not broad strokes. Can you recall where we landed with our problem description?

Client: Yeah. I'm afraid I may be fired at work because I don't clear my desk of all the clutter at the end of the day.

Therapist: Yes, that's excellent. It's specific, which makes it easier to begin to problem solve. After this pinpointing step, we talked about possible solutions to this problem, and you came up with three possible things you could do to address your worry about this problem. Do you remember those options?

Client: Yeah. First, I could do nothing and just try to let it go. Or I could talk to Mary, who works next to me, and ask her if she thought I could get fired for leaving the stuff in my desk basket. Or, I could talk to my boss about it and ask him if it was okay for me to leave papers in my basket overnight.

Therapist: Exactly. Those were the three possible solutions we talked about. Then we listed the pros and cons of each of these solutions and evaluated them. Do you recall the result of that process?

Client: Yeah. The option of talking to my boss had the most benefit to it and the least downside, from what I saw.

Therapist: Yeah, and that's where we ended last time. What I'd like to do now is work on implementing that solution. I can help rehearse the conversation in a role-play, here in the office. You willing to try that with me?

Client: I guess so. How do we go about doing it?

Therapist: Well, I'll play the role of your supervisor. What did you say his name is?

Client: Chuck Bailey.

(continued)

Therapist: Okay. I'll be Chuck Bailey and you play yourself. This will give you a chance at a dry run with this conversation and a way to reduce your anxiety over talking to him. So why don't you begin asking if you can talk to me briefly and we'll go from there.

Client: Okay. I'll give it a try. Chuck, could I talk to you privately for a minute?

Therapist: Sure. What's it about? Come on in and sit down.

Client: I want to ask a question that's been bothering me a little.

Therapist: Okay, what is it?

Client: Well, at night when I'm wrapping up my work . . . [cut to later]

Therapist: That was very good. How did you feel about it?

Client: Well, the first time was a little shaky, but by the third time we went through it, I felt good. I think I can do this tomorrow.

Therapist: Great! Can you remember to make a journal entry about your experience so we can go over it in our next session?

Client: Yeah, I can do that.

Therapist: Great! I'm looking forward to hearing what happened.

Critique of the Behavioral Strategies: Problem–Solving Therapy Demonstration Vignette

The following points were made in the critique:

a. Therapist begins by summarizing the steps of problem solving they have covered in previous sessions: pinpointing the problem, specifying possible solutions to the problem; listing and processing the pros and cons of each option; selecting one solution for implementation.

b. Role-played rehearsal of the chosen plan is used and is a common staple of CBT.

c. Therapist asks the client to record her experience of enacting this solution in real life; this is another example of using homework between sessions and then processing the material within the next session.

Additional points that could be made:

a. Role-play increases confidence and reduces anxiety in the client and allows any obstacles to be addressed via more problem solving.

b. Problem solving trains the client to be solution-oriented and not just problem-focused; it is empowering toward constructive action.

Comments you would like to make:

____

____

____

____

Homework: The homework assignment "Applying Problem-Solving to Interpersonal Conflict" (*Adult Psychotherapy Homework Planner*, 2nd ed., by Jongsma) is designed to help the client use classic problem-solving skills to find win-win solutions to conflicts. Behavioral activation is facilitated by assigning the exercise "Identify and Schedule Pleasant Activities" (see www.wiley.com/go/gadwb).

Behavioral Strategies Review

1. Name and describe two behavioral strategies that may be used in the treatment of GAD discussed in this section.

   CBT approaches employ other behavioral strategies such as behavioral activation and problem-solving skills training when treating GAD. In behavioral activation, clients are encouraged to identify pleasant, worthwhile, or self-concept-building activities that they can engage in on a daily basis. Such activities create pleasant circumstances for focused attention, build self-esteem, and generate positive affect counter to the anxious and depressed moods that often accompany worry.

   Problem-solving skills training is a common behavioral intervention used in CBT for many disorders. It teaches an orientation to problems that accepts that they will occur, as well as a systematic approach for addressing them. The primary steps involved in problem solving are as follows:

   1. Define the problem specifically.
   2. Generate options for addressing the problem.
   3. Evaluate the pros and cons of the generated solution options.
   4. Select the best solution and implement it.
   5. Evaluate the effectiveness of the plan.
   6. Keep, revise, or change the plan based on the evaluation of its effectiveness.

   Problem solving guides clients to address worries productively and counters the more ruminative habit characteristic of GAD. Homework assignments in which problem solving is implemented, recorded, and reviewed are commonly used.

Talking Points

Consider facilitating an exercise in problem solving. This can be launched with the question "What are some common clinical problems seen in GAD to which problem solving can be applied?" Participants can then be asked to take one or more identified problems through the steps in problem solving.

(continued)

- Examples of common problems could be drawn from these previously mentioned major categories:
  - Daily responsibilities (e.g., meeting deadlines, completing tasks)
  - Health of family members (e.g., will someone get sick)
  - Safety of children (e.g., at school, driving, health)
  - Finances (e.g., excessive expenses, more income)
  - Job security (e.g., job performance, getting a job)
  - Relationships (e.g., loss, finding one, conflicts)
- Basic steps in problem solving are:
  1. Define the problem specifically.
  2. Generate options that may help solve it.
  3. Evaluate the feasibility and likely effectiveness (pros and cons) of each option.
  4. Select an option based on the previous evaluation step and implement the option.
  5. Evaluate effectiveness of the option.
  6. Keep, revise, or change the plan based on the evaluation of its effectiveness.

Behavioral Strategies Review Test Question

1. When conceptualizing a problem to be subjected to problem solving, it is important to:

   A. Define it by using the first description that comes to mind
   B. Define it in specific behavioral terms
   C. Define it generally, so that it is more encompassing of all potential factors
   D. Simultaneously think of options for solving it

   Answer: B

Chapter References

Bernstein, D. A., & Thomas, D. B. (1973). *Progressive Relaxation Training: A Manual for the Helping Professions*. Champaign, IL: Research.

Finley, J. R., & Bret, A. M. (2011). *Veterans and Active Duty Military Psychotherapy Homework Planner*. Hoboken, NJ: Wiley.

Jongsma, A. E. (2006). *Adult Psychotherapy Homework Planner* (2nd ed.). Hoboken, NJ: Wiley.

Leahy, R. L. (2005). The Worry Cure: Seven Steps to Stop Worry from Stopping You. New York: Harmony.

Zinbarg, R. E., Michelle, G. C., & David, H. B. (1993). *Mastery of Your Anxiety and Worry: Therapist Guide*. New York: Psychological.

What Are Common Considerations for Relapse Prevention?

Chapter Review

1. What are the common considerations in relapse prevention?

---

1. Explain the rationale of relapse prevention interventions.
2. Distinguish between lapse and relapse.
3. Identify and rehearse managing high-risk situations for a lapse.
4. Encourage routine use of skills learned in therapy.
5. Consider developing a coping card.
6. Schedule periodic booster therapy sessions.

Table 6.1 Integrating Relapse Prevention Objectives and Interventions Into the Treatment Plan

Objectives	Interventions
13. Verbalize an understanding of relapse prevention and the difference between a lapse and relapse.	1. Provide a rationale for relapse prevention that discusses the risk and introduces strategies for preventing it. 2. Discuss with the client the distinction between a lapse and relapse, associating a lapse with a temporary setback and relapse with a return to a sustained pattern of thinking, feeling, and behaving that is characteristic of GAD.
14. Identify potential situations that could trigger a lapse and implement strategies to manage these situations.	1. Reviewing past anxiety-producing situations, assist the client in identifying future situations or circumstances in which lapses could occur. 2. Instruct the client to routinely use strategies learned in therapy (e.g., relaxation, cognitive restructuring, problem solving) to manage trigger situations, building them into his/her life as much as possible.

(continued)

Table 6.1   (Continued)

Objectives	Interventions
	3. Develop a coping card on which coping strategies and other important information can be kept (e.g., steps in problem solving, positive coping statements, reminders that were helpful to the client during therapy). 4. Schedule periodic maintenance or booster sessions to help the client maintain therapeutic gains and problem-solve challenges.

Chapter Review Test Question

1.   John and his therapist are talking about future situations that could challenge him and potentially set him back if he encounters one. They plan to review these encounters and develop a plan for coping with them in common sessions. Which consideration in relapse prevention is being conducted in the current session?

    A. Developing a coping card
    B. Distinguishing between a lapse and relapse
    C. Encouraging the routine use of skills learned in therapy
    D. Identifying high-risk situations for a lapse
    Answer: D

Talking Point

Select an example from the list of Common Considerations in Relapse Prevention and ask participants, "Why would this be important in helping a client prevent relapse?"

• Most answers are self-evident, except perhaps why distinguishing a lapse from a relapse is important. The rationale for the distinction is that lapses do not necessarily need to result in relapses if they can be caught and managed.

Closing Remarks and Resources

As we note on the DVD, it is important to be aware that the research support for any particular EST supports the identified treatment as it was delivered in the studies supporting it. The use of only selected objectives or interventions from ESTs may not be empirically supported.

If you want to incorporate an EST into your treatment plan, it should reflect the major objectives and interventions of the approach. Note that in addition to their primary objectives and interventions, many ESTs have options within them that may or may not be used depending on the client's need (e.g., skills training). Most treatment manuals, books, and other training programs identify the primary objectives and interventions used in the EST.

An existing resource for integrating research-supported treatments into treatment planning is the Practice*Planners*® series[1] of treatment planners. The series contains several books that have integrated goals, objectives, and interventions consistent with those of identified ESTs into treatment plans for several applicable problems and disorders:

- *The Severe and Persistent Mental Illness Treatment Planner*, 2nd ed. (Berghuis, Jongsma, & Bruce)
- *The Family Therapy Treatment Planner*, 2nd ed. (Dattilio, Jongsma, & Davis)
- *The Complete Adult Psychotherapy Treatment Planner*, 4th ed. (Jongsma, Peterson, & Bruce)
- *The Adolescent Psychotherapy Treatment Planner* (Jongsma, Peterson, McInnis, & Bruce)
- *The Child Psychotherapy Treatment Planner* (Jongsma, Peterson, McInnis, & Bruce)

---

[1] These books are updated frequently, check with the publisher for the latest editions and for further information about the Practice*Planners*®.

> *The Veterans and Active Duty Military Psychotherapy Treatment Planner* (Moore & Jongsma)
> *The Addiction Treatment Planner* (Perkinson, Jongsma, & Bruce)
> *The Couples Psychotherapy Treatment Planner*, 2nd ed. (O'Leary, Heyman, & Jongsma)
> *The Older Adult Psychotherapy Treatment Planner*, 2nd ed. (Frazer, Hinrichsen, & Jongsma)
> *The School Counseling and School Social Work Treatment Planner*, 2nd ed. (Knapp, Jongsma, & Dimmitt)
> *The Crisis Counseling and Traumatic Events Treatment Planner*, 2nd ed. (Kolski, Jongsma, & Myer)

Finally, it is important to remember that the purpose of this series is to demonstrate the process of evidence-based psychotherapy treatment planning for common mental health problems. It is designed to be informational in nature, and does not intend to be a substitute for clinical training in the interventions discussed and demonstrated. In accordance with ethical guidelines, therapists should have competency in the services they deliver.

A

A Sample Evidence-Based Treatment Plan for Generalized Anxiety Disorder

Primary Problem: Generalized Anxiety Disorder

Behavioral Definitions

1. Expresses excessive anxiety and worry that is difficult to control, occurring more days than not, for a period of at least six months, and is focused on several different events or activities.
2. Displays restlessness or verbalizes feeling on edge.
3. Exhibits a general state of irritability.
4. Displays and describes muscle tension.

Diagnosis: Generalized Anxiety Disorder (300.3)

Long-Term Goal

1. Reduce overall frequency, intensity, and duration of the anxiety so that daily functioning is not impaired.

Objectives	Interventions
1. Describe current and past experiences with the worry and anxiety symptoms, complete with their impact on functioning and attempts to resolve it.	1. Focus on developing a level of trust with the client; provide support and empathy to encourage the client to feel safe in expressing his/her GAD symptoms. 2. Ask the client to describe his/her past experiences of anxiety and their impact on functioning; assess the focus, excessiveness, and uncontrollability of the worry and the type, frequency, intensity, and duration of his/her anxiety symptoms (e.g., The Anxiety Disorders Interview Schedule for the DSM-IV by DiNardo, Brown, and Barlow).
2. Complete psychological tests designed to assess worry and anxiety symptoms.	1. Administer a self-report measure to help assess the nature and degree of the client's worry and anxiety symptoms (e.g., The Penn State Worry Questionnaire by Meyer, Miller, Metzger, and Borkovec) and the impact those symptoms have on functioning (e.g., OQ-45.2 by Lambert and Burlingame or the Symptom Checklist-90-R by Derogatis).

(continued)

Objectives	Interventions
3. Cooperate with an evaluation by a prescribing practitioner for psychotropic medication.	1. Refer the client to a prescribing practitioner for a psychotropic medication consultation. 2. Monitor the client's psychotropic medication compliance, side effects, and effectiveness; confer regularly with the prescribing practitioner.
4. Verbalize an understanding of the cognitive, physiological, and behavioral components of anxiety and its treatment.	1. Teach the client how generalized anxiety typically involves excessive worry about unrealistic threats, various bodily expressions of tension, overarousal, and hypervigilance, and avoidance of what is threatening that interact to maintain the problem (see *Mastery of Your Anxiety and Worry—Therapist Guide* by Craske, Barlow, and O'Leary). 2. Discuss how treatment targets worry, anxiety symptoms, and avoidance to help the client manage worry effectively and reduce overarousal and unnecessary avoidance.
5. Learn and implement calming skills to reduce overall anxiety and manage anxiety symptoms.	1. Teach the client relaxation skills (e.g., progressive muscle, imagery, diaphragmatic breathing, verbal cues for deep relaxation), how to discriminate better between relaxation and tension, as well as how to apply these skills to his/her daily life (e.g., see *Progressive Relaxation Training* by Bernstein and Borkovec; *Treating GAD* by Rygh and Sanderson). 2. Assign the client homework each session in which he/she practices relaxation exercises daily for at least 15 minutes; review, reinforcing success while providing corrective feedback toward improvement.
6. Learn and implement a strategy to limit the association between various environmental settings and worry, delaying the worry until a designated worry time.	1. Explain the rationale for using a worry time as well as how it is to be used; agree upon a worry time and place with the client and assign its implementation. 2. Teach the client how to recognize, stop, and delay worry until the agreed-upon worry time and place using skills such as thought stopping and relaxation.
7. Identify, challenge, and replace biased, worrisome self-talk and beliefs with positive, realistic, and empowering self-talk.	1. Explore the client's biased schema and self-talk that mediate his/her fear response; assist him/her in generating thoughts that correct for the biases; use behavioral experiments to test fearful versus alternative predictions. 2. Assign the client a homework exercise in which he or she identifies fearful self-talk, identifies biases in the self-talk, generates alternatives, and tests through behavioral experiments; review and reinforce success, providing corrective feedback toward improvement.

Objectives	Interventions
8. Learn and implement problem-solving strategies for realistically addressing worries.	1. Teach the client problem-solving strategies in which he or she takes a positive problem orientation and utilizes problem-solving steps to address problems, including defining and pinpointing the problem, developing a list of possible solutions, analyzing and comparing the pros and cons of each solution, selecting and implementing a solution, analyzing the solution for effectiveness, and adjusting the action if necessary for mutual satisfaction. 2. Assign the client a homework exercise in which he or she implements problem-solving skills for a current problem (see "Applying Problem-Solving to Interpersonal Conflict" in *Adult Psychotherapy Homework Planner*, 2nd ed., by Jongsma; *Mastery of Your Anxiety and Worry—Client Guide* by Zinbarg, Craske, Barlow, and O'Leary; or *Generalized Anxiety Disorder* by Brown, O'Leary, and Barlow); review, reinforcing success and providing corrective feedback toward improvement.
9. Verbalize an understanding of relapse prevention and the difference between a lapse and relapse.	1. Provide a rationale for relapse prevention that discusses the risk and introduces strategies for preventing it. 2. Discuss with the client the distinction between a lapse and relapse, associating a lapse with a temporary setback and relapse with a return to a sustained pattern of thinking, feeling, and behaving that is characteristic of GAD.
10. Identify potential situations that could trigger a lapse and implement strategies to manage these situations.	1. Identify and rehearse with the client the management of future situations or circumstances in which lapses could occur. 2. Instruct the client to routinely use strategies learned in therapy (e.g., behavioral activation, cognitive restructuring, problem solving), building them into his/her life as much as possible. 3. Schedule periodic maintenance or booster sessions to help the client maintain therapeutic gains and problem-solve challenges.

B

Chapter Review Test Questions and Answers Explained

Chapter 1: What Is Generalized Anxiety Disorder?

1. Which of the following best describes the primary diagnostic feature of Generalized Anxiety Disorder (GAD)?

   A. Excessive worry specifically about being humiliated in public
   B. Excessive worry about several everyday or real-life problems
   C. Excessive worry about having a specific disease
   D. Excessive worry specifically about having an unexpected panic attack

      A. *Incorrect*: GAD is characterized by excessive worry about several everyday or real-life problems. This specific worry is more likely to be seen in social anxiety disorder.

      B. *Correct*: This is the best answer as GAD is characterized by excessive worry about several everyday or real-life problems.

      C. *Incorrect*: GAD is characterized by excessive worry about several everyday or real-life problems. This specific worry is more likely to be seen in hypochondriasis.

      D. *Incorrect*: GAD is characterized by excessive worry about several everyday or real-life problems. This specific worry is more likely to be seen in panic disorder.

2. True or false? According to the *DSM*, you can diagnose Generalized Anxiety Disorder when only the excessive worry criteria are met; that is, without any evidence of physiological overarousal.

   False. Both criteria need to be met to make the diagnosis. In *DSM-IV-TR*, this requires the presence of at least three of the following symptoms of overarousal:

   ➤ Restlessness or feeling keyed up or on edge
   ➤ Being easily fatigued

> ➢ Difficulty concentrating or going blank
> ➢ Irritability
> ➢ Muscle tension
> ➢ Sleep disturbance

It may be of interest to note that the number of these physiological symptoms required to make this diagnosis may be reduced in the upcoming revision to the *DSM*.

Chapter 2: What Are the Six Steps in Building a Treatment Plan?

1. Some patients with Generalized Anxiety Disorder (GAD) may worry about finances or job security. Others may worry about their children or deadlines. Some may have a sleep disturbance, whereas others may not. In which step of treatment planning would you record the particular expressions of GAD for your individual client?

   A. Creating short-term objectives
   B. Describing the problem's manifestations
   C. Identifying the primary problem
   D. Selecting treatment interventions

      A. *Incorrect*: Expressions of the disorder, also referred to as manifestations, features, or symptoms, are described in Step 2 of treatment planning. They are not objectives for the client to achieve.
      B. *Correct*: Expressions of the disorder, also referred to as manifestations, features, or symptoms, are described in Step 2 of treatment planning.
      C. *Incorrect*: Expressions of the disorder, also referred to as manifestations, features, or symptoms, are described in Step 2 of treatment planning. They are expressions of the primary problem—generalized anxiety disorder.
      D. *Incorrect*: Expressions of the disorder, also referred to as manifestations, features, or symptoms, are described in Step 2 of treatment planning. They are not interventions that the therapist will use to help the client achieve his or her objectives.

2. The statement "Learn and implement problem-solving skills to address worries in a more productive manner" is an example of a statement describing which of the following elements of a psychotherapy treatment plan?

   A. A primary problem
   B. A short-term objective
   C. A symptom manifestation
   D. A treatment intervention

A. *Incorrect*: The primary problem (Step 1 in treatment planning) is the summary description, usually in diagnostic terms, of the client's primary problem.

B. *Correct*: This is a short-term objective (Step 5 in treatment planning). It describes a desired action of the client that is likely to help him or her reach a treatment goal.

C. *Incorrect*: Symptom manifestations (Step 2 in treatment planning) describe the client's particular expression (i.e., features or symptoms) of the primary problem.

D. *Incorrect*: A treatment intervention (Step 6 in treatment planning) describes the therapist's actions designed to help the client achieve his or her short-term objectives.

Chapter 3: What Is the Brief History of the EST Movement?

1. Which statement best describes the process used to identify ESTs?

    A. Consumers of mental health services nominated therapies.
    B. Experts came to a consensus based on their experiences with the treatments.
    C. Researchers submitted their works.
    D. Task groups reviewed the literature using clearly defined selection criteria for ESTs.

    A. *Incorrect*: Mental health professionals selected ESTs.
    B. *Incorrect*: Expert consensus was not the method used to identify ESTs.
    C. *Incorrect*: Empirical works in the existing literature were reviewed to identify ESTs.
    D. *Correct*: Review groups consisting of mental health professionals selected ESTs based on predetermined criteria such as *well-established* and *probably efficacious*.

2. Based on the differences in their criteria, in which of the following ways are *well-established* treatments different from those classified as *probably efficacious*?

    A. Only *probably efficacious* allowed the use of single-case design experiments.
    B. Only *well-established* allowed studies comparing the treatment to a psychological placebo.
    C. Only *well-established* required demonstration by at least two different, independent investigators or investigating teams.
    D. Only *well-established* allowed studies comparing the treatment to a pill placebo.

A. *Incorrect*: Both sets of criteria allowed use of single-subject designs. *Well-established* required a larger series than did *probably efficacious* (see II under Well-Established and III under Probably Efficacious).

B. *Incorrect*: Studies using comparison to psychological placebos were acceptable in both sets of criteria (see IA under Well-Established and II under Probably Efficacious).

C. *Correct*: One of the primary differences between treatments classified as *well-established* and those classified as *probably efficacious* is that *well-established* therapies have had their efficacy demonstrated by at least two different, independent investigators (see V under Well-Established).

D. *Incorrect*: Studies using comparison to pill placebos were acceptable in both sets of criteria (see IA under Well-Established and II under Probably Efficacious).

Chapter 4: What Are the Identified Empirically Supported Treatments for Generalized Anxiety Disorder?

1. Treatments based on the principles of which of the following therapeutic models have been identified by reviewers and evidence-based practice guideline developers (e.g., the National Institute for Health and Clinical Excellence) as having strong research support for the treatment of generalized anxiety disorder (GAD)?

   A. Cognitive-behavioral therapy
   B. Interpersonal therapy
   C. Psychoanalytic therapy
   D. Psychodynamic therapy

   A. *Correct*: Treatments based on the principles of cognitive-behavioral therapy (CBT) have been identified as having the highest level of empirical support for the treatment of GAD, based on the reviewers and guideline developers discussed in the chapter.

   B. *Incorrect*: Interpersonal therapy, which has a supportive evidence base for the treatment of depression and specific eating disorders, has not been recognized as having a similar level of efficacy for the treatment of GAD, based on the reviewers and guideline developers discussed in the chapter.

   C. *Incorrect*: Psychoanalytic therapy has not been recognized as having an evidence base similar to that of CBT for the treatment of GAD, based on the reviewers and guideline developers discussed in the chapter.

   D. *Incorrect*: Psychoanalytic therapy has not been recognized as having an evidence base similar to that of CBT for the treatment of GAD, based on the reviewers and guideline developers discussed in the chapter.

2. As discussed in the chapter, the worry time intervention used in some forms of CBT for GAD is categorized under which of the following classes or types of interventions?

   A. Cognitive restructuring
   B. Problem solving
   C. Relaxation training
   D. Stimulus control

      A. *Incorrect*: Although cognitive restructuring techniques may be used during the worry time to address worries more productively, worry time is based on a stimulus control rationale.
      B. *Incorrect*: Although problem-solving skills may be used during the worry time to address worries more productively, worry time is based on a stimulus control rationale.
      C. *Incorrect*: Although relaxation skills may be used during the worry time to address worries more productively, worry time is based on a stimulus control rationale.
      D. *Correct*: The rationale for the use of worry time is that worry in GAD occurs in many environmental contexts and therefore is under poor stimulus control. Postponing it to a specific time and place, even though clients may be asked to address it using therapeutic skills, is intended to bring it under better stimulus control.

Chapter 5: How Do You Integrate ESTs Into Treatment Planning?

Assessment/Psychoeducation

1. At what point in therapy is psychoeducation conducted?

   A. At the end of therapy
   B. During the assessment phase
   C. During the initial treatment session
   D. Throughout therapy

      A. *Incorrect*: Although some psychoeducation may be done at this phase of therapy, psychoeducation is conducted throughout therapy.
      B. *Incorrect*: Although some psychoeducation is commonly done at assessment, psychoeducation is conducted throughout therapy.
      C. *Incorrect*: Although it is common for psychoeducation to be done early in therapy, it continues throughout.
      D. *Correct*: Psychoeducation permeates all phases of therapy.

Cognitive–Behavioral Therapy: Relaxation Training

1. As discussed in the chapter, what is the rationale for having a therapist consider teaching various methods of relaxation to a client as opposed to just one?

    A. Because all types of relaxation techniques have demonstrated efficacy in the treatment of GAD.
    B. Because it allows for flexibility of use and because clients may vary in which types of relaxation techniques they find effective.
    C. Because using multiple types of relaxation relaxes the client more than using one.
    D. Because using one type of relaxation does not relax the client as well as using many.
        A. *Incorrect*: Although applied relaxation has demonstrated efficacy as a stand-alone treatment, not all relaxation techniques have demonstrated efficacy in this manner. The rationale for teaching various methods is explained in answer B.
        B. *Correct*: As with any skills training, training more than one option allows for flexibility of use, and because clients may vary in which types of relaxation techniques they find effective.
        C. *Incorrect*: There is no evidence that using multiple types of relaxation techniques has an additive effect on the relaxation response. Any one type of relaxation training technique may work well with any one client. The rationale for teaching various methods is explained in answer B.
        D. *Incorrect*: This is the converse of answer C and is incorrect for similar reasons: Any one type of relaxation training technique may work well with any one client. The rationale for teaching various methods is explained in answer B.

Stimulus Control/Worry Time

1. Which of the following statements best describes an objective of the worry time procedure?

    A. To have a common language between the therapist and client: When one is worrying, both call that the worry time
    B. To postpone worries to a specific time and place where they can be addressed productively
    C. To recognize that whenever one is worrying, it is time to address it productively

D. To recognize that whenever one is worrying, the environmental stimulus causing it needs to be identified

    A. *Incorrect*: Although having a common language is helpful to therapeutic communication, this is not what worry time refers to, nor is it its purpose.

    B. *Correct*: Worry time is intended to bring worries under stimulus control (paired with as few environmental stimuli as possible) and provide the client with an opportunity to address the worries productively.

    C. *Incorrect*: Although the worry time procedure involves addressing worries productively, it does not recommend doing that whenever they appear, but rather at a specific time and place so as to bring it under stimulus control (paired with as few environmental stimuli as possible).

    D. *Incorrect*: Although it may be helpful to know if certain environmental stimuli seem to be eliciting worries reliably, it is not the intent of the worry time procedure to identify them. Rather, the intent is to bring worries under stimulus control (paired with as few environmental stimuli as possible) and provide the client with an opportunity to address the worries productively.

Cognitive–Behavioral Therapy: Cognitive Restructuring

1. Through discussions with her therapist, Jan comes to understand that her anxious feelings escalate when she is thinking worrisome thoughts about not getting her children's lunches made on time. This represents what process in cognitive therapy?

    A. Identifying the connection between thought and emotion

    B. Identifying the biases contained in self-talk

    C. Monitoring self-talk

    D. Shifting from biased to alternative beliefs and predictions

        A. *Correct*: The vignette describes a client learning how thoughts influence emotions.

        B. *Incorrect*: The vignette does not describe the biases evident in the anxiety-provoking thoughts.

        C. *Incorrect*: Monitoring is a recording of self-talk typically done by the client before demonstrating its connection to feelings, identifying biases in it, and testing it against alternatives.

        D. *Incorrect*: The vignette does not describe a shift in thinking or belief, only how the client is learning the connection between thoughts and feelings.

Cognitive–Behavioral Therapy: Exposure Therapy

1. One form of exposure that may be used in the treatment of generalized anxiety disorder is self-control desensitization. Which of the following best describes this procedure?

    A. Clients deliberately approach actual anxiety-provoking or worrisome situations while using skills learned in therapy to manage their reaction.
    B. Clients repeatedly imagine anxiety-provoking or worrisome situations while imagining themselves coping successfully by using relaxation and other newly learned skills.
    C. Clients repeatedly pair a relaxing word with a state of relaxation.
    D. Clients learn how to relax rapidly and then apply this skill in various actual anxiety-provoking or worrisome situations.
        A. *Incorrect*: This describes exposure in vivo—to actual anxiety-provoking or worrisome situations. Self-control desensitization is a form of imaginal exposure described in answer B.
        B. *Correct*: This describes self-control desensitization, which pairs in imagination anxiety-provoking or worrisome situations and successful coping.
        C. *Incorrect*: This describes cue-control relaxation, in which relaxation is paired with a word or phrase that is calming to the client. Self-controlled desensitization is a form of imaginal exposure described in answer B.
        D. *Incorrect*: This describes applied relaxation, in which relaxation is applied in actual anxiety-provoking or worrisome situations. Self-control desensitization is a form of imaginal exposure described in answer B.

Cognitive–Behavioral Therapy: Behavioral Strategies

1. When conceptualizing a problem to be subjected to problem solving, it is important to:

    A. Define it by using the first description that comes to mind
    B. Define it in specific behavioral terms
    C. Define it generally, so that it is more encompassing of all potential factors
    D. Simultaneously think of options for solving it
        A. *Incorrect*: The first step in problem solving is to define the problem specifically. A definition derived spontaneously, as described in A, may be specific or nonspecific.
        B. *Correct*: The first step in problem solving is to define the problem in specifics (e.g., the reports from that office are routinely late). Overly general definitions of problems makes them more difficult to solve (e.g., that office is lazy).

C. *Incorrect*: As noted in B above, an overly general definition of a problem makes it more difficult to solve (e.g., Specific: "I have trouble initiating conversations." Nonspecific: "I'm shy.").

D. *Incorrect*: Generating options for solving a problem comes after first defining it specifically.

Chapter 6: What Are Considerations for Relapse Prevention?

1. John and his therapist are talking about future situations that could challenge him and potentially set him back if he encounters one. They plan to review these encounters and develop a plan for coping with them in common sessions. Which consideration in relapse prevention is being conducted in the current session?

   A. Developing a coping card
   B. Distinguishing between a lapse and relapse
   C. Encouraging the routine use of skills learned in therapy
   D. Identifying high-risk situations for a lapse
      A. *Incorrect*: John may use a coping card to help him remember the skills learned in therapy that he will use to manage the high-risk situations being identified in this vignette.
      B. *Incorrect*: This is a psychoeducational intervention designed in part to help prevent misinterpretation of potentially manageable setbacks as an unmanageable relapse.
      C. *Incorrect*: John may use the skills learned in therapy to manage the high-risk situations being identified in this vignette.
      D. *Correct*: The vignette describes identifying high-risk situations for a lapse. John and his therapist will then review them and develop a plan for managing each one. They may rehearse the plan in session and/or through between-session exercises.

STUDY PACKAGE
CONTINUING EDUCATION
CREDIT INFORMATION

Evidence-Based Treatment Planning for Generalized Anxiety Disorder

Our goal is to provide you with current, accurate and practical information from the most experienced and knowledgeable speakers and authors.

Listed below are the continuing education credit(s) currently available for this self-study package. *Please note: Your state licensing board dictates whether self study is an acceptable form of continuing education. Please refer to your state rules and regulations.*

Counselors: CMI Education Institute, Inc. is an approved provider of the National Board of Certified Counselors, NBCC Provider #: 5637. We adhere to NBCC Continuing Education Guidelines. This self-study package qualifies for **3.0** contact hours.

Social Workers: CMI Education Institute, Inc., #1062, is approved as a provider for social work continuing education by the Association of Social Work Boards (ASWB), 400 South Ridge Parkway, Suite B, Culpeper VA 22701. www.aswb.org. CMI Education Institute, Inc. maintains responsibility for the program. Licensed Social Workers should contact their regulatory board to determine course approval. Social Workers will receive **3.0** (clinical) continuing education clock hours for completing this self-study package. Course Level: All Levels.

Marriage and Family Therapists: This activity consists of **3.0** hours of continuing education instruction. Credit requirements and approvals vary per state board regulations. Please save the course outline, the certificate of completion you receive from this self-study activity and contact your state board or organization to determine specific filing requirements.

Psychologists: CMI Education Institute, Inc. is approved by the American Psychological Association to sponsor continuing education for psychologists. CMI maintains responsibility for this program and its content. CMI is offering these self-study materials for **3.0** hours of continuing education credit.

Addiction Counselors: CMI Education Institute, Inc. is an approved provider of continuing education by the National Association of Alcoholism & Drug Abuse Counselors (NAADAC), provider #: 00131. This self-study package qualifies for **3.5** contact hours.

Nurses/Nurse Practitioners/Clinical Nurse Specialists: This activity meets the criteria for an American Nurses Credentialing Center (ANCC) Activity CMI Education Institute, Inc. is an approved sponsor by the American Psychological Association, which is recognized by the ANCC for behavioral health related activities.

This self-study activity qualifies for **3.0** contact hours.

Other Professions: This activity qualifies for **3.25** clock hours of instructional content as required by many national, state and local licensing boards and professional organizations. Retain your certificate of completion and contact your board or organization for specific filing requirements.

Procedures:

1. Review the materials (publication and DVD).

2. If seeking credit, complete the posttest/evaluation form:

-Complete posttest/evaluation in entirety; including your email address for the most prompt receipt of your certificate ofcompletion.

-Upon completion, mail to the address listed on the form along with the CE fee stated on the test. Tests will not be processed without the CE fee included.

Completed posttests must be received 6 months from the date of purchase. Your completed posttest/evaluation will be graded. If you receive a passing score (70% and above), you will be emailed/faxed/mailed a certificate of successful completion with earned continuing education credits. (Please include your email address on the posttest/ evaluation form for fastest response) If you do not pass the posttest, you will be sent a letter via email indicating areas of deficiency, and another posttest to complete. The posttest must be resubmitted and receive a passing grade before credit can be awarded. We will allow you to re-take as many times as necessary (with no additional fee) to receive a passing grade.

If you have any questions, please feel free to contact our customer service department at 1.800.844.8260.

CMI Education Institute

A Non-Profit Organization Connecting Knowledge with Need Since 1979

CMI Education PO BOX 1000 Eau Claire, WI 54702-1000

CMI Education Institute
A Non-Profit Organization Connecting Knowledge with Need Since 1979

Evidence-Based Treatment Planning
for Generalized Anxiety Disorder

Any persons interested in receiving credit may photocopy this form, complete and return with a payment of $15.00 per person CE fee. A certificate of successful completion will be sent to you. To receive your certificate sooner than two weeks, rush processing is available for a fee of $10. Please attach check or include credit card information below.

<table>
<tr><td colspan="2">For office use only</td></tr>
<tr><td>Rcvd.</td><td>__________</td></tr>
<tr><td>Graded</td><td>__________</td></tr>
<tr><td>Cert. sent</td><td>__________</td></tr>
</table>

Mail to: PESI, PO Box 1000, Eau Claire, WI 54702 or fax to PESI (800) 554-9775 (both sides)

CE Fee: $15: (Rush processing fee: $10)   **Total to be charged** ____________________

Credit Card #: ____________________________   **Exp Date:** ____________   **V-Code*:** __________

(*MC/VISA/Discover: last 3-digit # on signature panel on back of card.) (*American Express: 4-digit # above account # on face of card.)

Name (please print): ________________________ ________________________ ____________
                            LAST   FIRST   M.I.

Address: ____________________________ Daytime Phone: ____________________________

City: ____________________________ State: ____________ Zip Code: ____________

Signature: ____________________________ Email: ____________________________

Date Completed: ____________ Actual time (# of hours) taken to complete this offering: ______hours

Program Objectives After completing this publication, I have been able to achieve these objectives:

Explain the process and criteria for diagnosing generalized anxiety disorder	Yes	No
List the six steps in building a psychotherapy treatment plan	Yes	No
Examine how empirically supported treatments for generalized anxiety disorder have been identified	Yes	No
Illustrate objectives and treatment interventions consistent with those of identified empirically supported treatments for generalized anxiety disorder	Yes	No
Describe how to construct a psychotherapy treatment plan and inform it with objectives and treatment interventions identified empirically supported treatments for generalized anxiety disorder	Yes	No
Identify common considerations in the prevention of relapse of generalized anxiety disorder	Yes	No

Participant Profile:

1. Job Title: ____________________________ Employment setting: ____________________________

CMI Education
PO BOX 1000
Eau Claire, WI 54702-1000

ZNT044590

CE Release Date: 2/09/2012

Posttest Questions

1. According to psychiatric diagnostic classification systems, which of the following best describes the cognitive features characteristic of generalized anxiety disorder?
   A. Excessive worry about delusional concerns
   B. Excessive worry about everyday concerns
   C. Excessive worry about having panic attacks
   D. Excessive worry about one's health

2. In addition to the excessive worry characteristic of generalized anxiety disorder, which of following diagnostic criteria must also be met to make this diagnosis?
   A. An inability to use problem-solving skills to address worries
   B. An inability to relax
   C. At least three of six symptoms reflecting increased physiological arousal
   D. Avoidance of least three feared objects or situations

3. A patient's expression of generalized anxiety disorder may include excessive worry about finances, difficulty sleeping, and irritability among other symptoms. In which of the following steps in the treatment planning process discussed in this program would these features be recorded?
   A. Creating short-term objectives
   B. Describing the problem's manifestations
   C. Selecting therapeutic interventions
   D. Specifying long-term goals

4. As discussed in this program, which of the following requirements was unique to APA Division 12's criteria for a well-established treatment, differentiating it from lesser levels of evidence such as probably efficacious?
   A. Independent replication of efficacy studies was required.
   B. Use of pill placebos in efficacy studies was required.
   C. Use of psychological placebos in efficacy studies was required.
   D. Use of random assignment in efficacy studies was required.

5. According to several reviewers of the psychotherapy outcome literature cited in this program, which of the following interventions has the highest level of evidence supporting its efficacy in the treatment of generalized anxiety disorder?
   A. Cognitive behavioral therapy
   B. Family therapy
   C. Interpersonal therapy
   D. Psychoanalytic therapy

6. A treatment plan for generalized anxiety disorder (GAD) has the following therapeutic intervention statement: "Discuss the nature of GAD, how the treatment model conceptualizes its development and maintenance, and the rationale for the treatment approach." This statement is characteristic of the following interventions used in cognitive behavioral therapy for GAD?
   A. Cognitive restructuring
   B. Exposure therapy
   C. Psychoeducation
   D. Relaxation training

7. According to this program, which of the following is the primary rationale for using the intervention called "worry time," in which the client is taught how to postpone thinking about worries until a specified place and time a day?
   A. To bring worries under better "stimulus control"
   B. To learn how to stop thinking about worries

CMI Education
PO BOX 1000
Eau Claire, WI 54702-1000

C. To reduce distraction caused by worries
D. To reduce tension caused by worries

8. According to this program, a common practice in relapse prevention plans is to identify high-risk situations for a lapse and rehearse using skills learned in therapy to manage them.
    A. TRUE
    B. FALSE

9. True or False: According to this program, interventions commonly used in cognitive behavioral therapies for generalized anxiety disorder include psychoeducation, relaxation training, and cognitive restructuring.
    A. TRUE
    B. FALSE

10. Which of the following best describes the approach to creating an evidence-based treatment plan for eating disorders that is recommended in this program?
    A. The therapist conducts cognitive therapy.
    B. The therapist conducts relaxation training.
    C. The therapist incorporates into therapy the objectives and interventions consistent with research-supported treatments.
    D. The therapist incorporates into therapy the use of an objective measure of the eating disorder to track treatment progress.

11. If an individual's worry is a feature of another current psychiatric disorder (e.g., someone with obsessive compulsive disorder worrying about contamination), this worry also counts toward meeting the criteria for generalized anxiety disorder?
    A. TRUE
    B. FALSE

12. Which of the following statements is true regarding the gender distribution of those diagnosed with generalized anxiety disorder?
    A. It occurs equally among men and women.
    B. It occurs exclusively in women.
    C. It occurs more in men than women.
    D. It occurs more in women than men.

13. A therapist decides to include relaxation training as part of the treatment plan for her client with generalized anxiety disorder. In which of the following steps in the treatment planning process should this be recorded?
    A. Creating short-term objectives
    B. Describing the problem's manifestations
    C. Selecting therapeutic interventions
    D. Specifying long-term goals

14. A treatment plan contains the sentence, "Consistently uses alcohol or other mood-altering drugs until high, intoxicated, or passed out." In which of the following steps in the treatment planning process would this be recorded?
    A. Creating short-term objectives
    B. Describing the problem's manifestations
    C. Selecting therapeutic interventions
    D. Specifying long-term goals

CMI Education
PO BOX 1000
Eau Claire, WI 54702-1000

Posttest Questions Continued

15. A treatment plan for generalized anxiety disorder (GAD) has the following short-term objective for the client: "Identify, challenge and change self-talk that increases anxiety and precludes effective problem-solving." This statement is characteristic of the following interventions commonly used in cognitive behavioral therapy for GAD?
    A. Cognitive restructuring
    B. Exposure therapy
    C. Psychoeducation
    D. Relaxation training

16. According to this program, which of the following best describes the first step in effective problem-solving?
    A. Define how the problem could be solved.
    B. Define one's emotional response to the problem.
    C. Define the problem generally.
    D. Define the problem specifically.

17. According to this program, behavioral activation, a common technique used in the behavioral treatment of depression, is used in some applications of cognitive behavioral therapy for generalized anxiety disorder.
    A. TRUE
    B. FALSE

18. A therapist discovers that his client with generalized anxiety disorder fears and avoids specific anxiety-provoking situations. He plans with the client homework exercises in which the client will intentionally approach these feared situations while using his newly acquired coping strategies to manage the situation. Which of the following therapeutic techniques is the therapist prescribing in this example?
    A. Behavioral activation
    B. Exposure therapy
    C. Problem-solving skills training
    D. Relaxation training

19. According to this program, the American Psychological Association defines an evidence-based practice as the integration of the best available research with clinical expertise in the context of patient characteristics, culture, and preferences.
    A. TRUE
    B. FALSE

20. In identifying the evidence-based treatments cited in this program, the authors (i.e., Jongsma & Bruce) have used which of the following methods?
    A. Establishing their own specific criteria for research support and citing those treatments that meet them
    B. Identifying patterns of agreement across reviewers, review groups, and evidence-based practice guideline developers
    C. Identifying treatments most preferred by patients/client
    D. Identifying treatments most preferred by therapists